Introducti

The **landscape of North Wales** conta many ancient hillforts. Most were built by our ancestors until the Romans occu remained in use during the Roman period. These settlements vary greatly in size, elevation, complexity and location. Many were built on land with natural steep slopes, often at strategic points overlooking valleys. They were defended by deep ditches and ramparts made mainly of earth but sometimes stone, generally topped with a large wooden palisade. Built over 2,500 years ago with primitive tools the larger hillforts are an amazing feat of engineering and collective human endeavour. Within the ramparts people generally lived in simple wooden framed roundhouses with wattle and daub walls and a central hearth under a thatched roof. Iron Age people were farmers, traders, skilled craftsmen as well as warriors.

The building of hillforts represented a significant cultural change in pre-historic times, but their role in a largely farming society remains unclear and they may have served different purposes. Undoubtedly their defences offered protection to community and family groups at times of tribal warfare or threat. Some may have been tribal centres which controlled the surrounding countryside and nearby markets and symbolized power and status. Others, defensively weak and with little evidence of continuous occupation, may have been used seasonally for trading, ceremonial purposes and religious celebrations. What is not in doubt is that hillforts are evocative man-made monuments to our past that adorn the beautiful North Wales landscape, generally offering panoramic views.

This book of 30 walks explores the diversity of hillfort sites in North Wales, from the impressive chain of hillforts on the Clwydian Range to more remote and less well known ones elsewhere. Included is Tre'r Ceiri, on the Llŷn Peninsula, one of the best preserved hillforts in Britain. The routes, which range from an easy 1 mile waymarked trail to a more challenging 10 mile upland valley walk in Snowdonia. They follow public rights of way or permissive paths, or cross Open Access land.

Be suitably prepared and equipped, especially on higher routes. Walking boots are recommended, along with appropriate clothing to protect against the elements. The condition of the paths can vary according to season and weather! Refer any rights of way problems encountered to the relevant County Council.

Each walk has a detailed map and description which enables the route to be followed without difficulty, but be aware that changes in detail can occur at any time. The location of each walk is shown on the back cover and a summary of the key features of each is provided. This includes an estimated walking time, but allow more time to enjoy the scenery. Please observe the country code and respect any hillfort site visited.

Enjoy your walking!

MOEL Y GAER

DESCRIPTION An undulating 4 mile (**A**) or 2½ mile (**B**) walk from a small village on Halkyn Mountain in Flintshire. The route features attractive countryside, a small lake, a section of Wat's Dyke Way and at the end a delightful circuit of the ramparts of Moel y Gaer Iron-Age hillfort, offering panoramic all-round views. It incorporates sections of the medieval trading route from Chester to Denbigh, used by travellers and pack ponies, later becoming part of the London-Holyhead Post road, and a section of the old Chester-Holywell coaching road. Allow about 2½ hours.

START Rhosesmor [SJ 214684]

DIRECTIONS Rhosesmor lies on the B5123, accessed from the A541 from Mold. In the village turn off the B5123 to park on a side road near a childrens' play area.

*M**oel y Gaer hillfort stands above the village of Rhosesmor, at a height of 994 feet, the highest point of Halkyn Mountain, a narrow upland plateau of carboniferous limestone. It is 600 feet in diameter, with entrance, guard chambers, ramparts and ditches. Excavations undertaken in 1972-74 during the construction of a storage reservoir within the fort, revealed evidence of earlier Neolithic and Bronze Age occupation. Remains of both round and rectangular buildings indicate three phases of development. Also found was the site of a fire beacon built in 1814 to warn of any French threat from the sea during the war with Napoleon. It is said that in 1403, Hywel Gwynedd set up a camp on the hill during his support of Owain Glyndŵr's revolt.*

*H**alkyn Mountain has been exploited for lead from Romans times until the 1980s. During the 18th and 19th centuries it became a major lead producer, with large scale deep mines replacing shallow workings. Beneath Rhosesmor is a large cavern about 150 feet high, containing two lakes of clear blue water, over 200 feet deep. It was discovered in 1932 by Capt. Jack Francis, a mining engineer, who had to rescue two men, whose makeshift raft collapsed whilst surveying the lakes. In 1937, a raft made of empty oil barrels being used by geologists inspecting the lakes, similarly capsized. Fortunately only their pride was hurt.*

I Continue along the road, and after about ¹/₃ mile, on a bend, take a signposted path to a stile ahead. Keep ahead to cross another stile, then follow the hedge on your left – *with good views across the Dee estuary* – down to cross a stile. Descend to a stile/gate, then go up the field to a gate and across the next to a stile/gate. Go half-LEFT down to a tree boundary corner. Keep the boundary on your left to cross a hidden stile in it before the field corner. Turn RIGHT along the field edge to a stile onto a road. Follow it LEFT to a junction by a house. Turn LEFT along Middle Mill Road – *the medieval trading route* – to the next junction by a farm. (For **Walk B** continue along the road to point 4.)

2 Cross a stile on the right and go down the field to a gate and across the next undulating field to a stile beyond a telegraph pole. Follow the power cables across the next field and down to a stile at the end of a wood and a sleeper bridge beyond. Go half-LEFT to steps at a gap in the tree boundary onto a narrow enclosed green track. Turn LEFT to a nearby finger post, where you join Wat's Dyke Way. Follow the signed path to Berth Ddu along the narrow green track past the wood and on to reach a road by a house. Follow it ahead. *The track and road are part of the old coach road which ran from Chester via Halkyn to Holywell, until its replacement by the original A55 built in 1826-7.*

3 Shortly turn LEFT on a signposted path up Midlist farm's driveway, passing through what was a large park until the early 18thC. Just before it begins to bend left, angle RIGHT on the waymarked path. It follows telegraph poles up the edge of a small wood to a stile, then up a field – *with great views looking back* – to another stile, and along the next field edge to a further stile. Descend to another below, then just beyond turn LEFT alongside the tree/hedge bound-

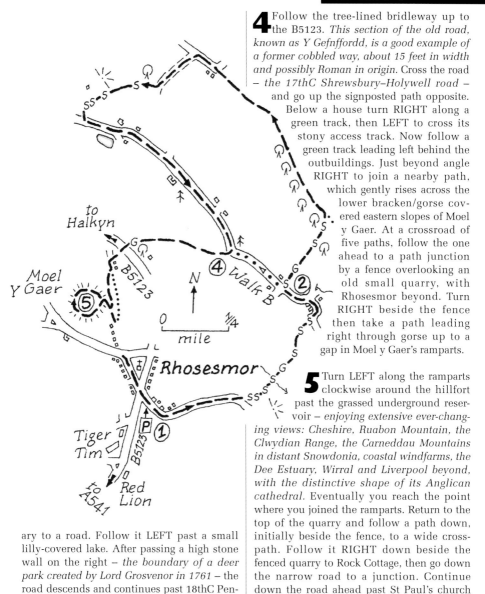

4 Follow the tree-lined bridleway up to the B5123. *This section of the old road, known as Y Gefnffordd, is a good example of a former cobbled way, about 15 feet in width and possibly Roman in origin.* Cross the road – the 17thC Shrewsbury–Holywell road – and go up the signposted path opposite. Below a house turn RIGHT along a green track, then LEFT to cross its stony access track. Now follow a green track leading left behind the outbuildings. Just beyond angle RIGHT to join a nearby path, which gently rises across the lower bracken/gorse covered eastern slopes of Moel y Gaer. At a crossroad of five paths, follow the one ahead to a path junction by a fence overlooking an old small quarry, with Rhosesmor beyond. Turn RIGHT beside the fence then take a path leading right through gorse up to a gap in Moel y Gaer's ramparts.

5 Turn LEFT along the ramparts clockwise around the hillfort past the grassed underground reservoir – *enjoying extensive ever-changing views: Cheshire, Ruabon Mountain, the Clwydian Range, the Carneddau Mountains in distant Snowdonia, coastal windfarms, the Dee Estuary, Wirral and Liverpool beyond, with the distinctive shape of its Anglican cathedral.* Eventually you reach the point where you joined the ramparts. Return to the top of the quarry and follow a path down, initially beside the fence, to a wide crosspath. Follow it RIGHT down beside the fenced quarry to Rock Cottage, then go down the narrow road to a junction. Continue down the road ahead past St Paul's church to the B5123 and along the road opposite to the start.

ary to a road. Follow it LEFT past a small lilly-covered lake. After passing a high stone wall on the right – *the boundary of a deer park created by Lord Grosvenor in 1761* – the road descends and continues past 18thC Pen-y-Parc. Later, on a bend turn RIGHT along a signposted bridleway.

WALK 2

MOEL HIRADDUG

DESCRIPTION A 6¼ mile walk (**A**) across undulating countryside, featuring two old water-mills, the 16thC Blue Lion Inn in Cwm, and a short climb to explore the delightful limestone hill of Moel Hiraddug (869 ft/265 metres) crowned by a hillfort, offering panoramic views. Allow about 4 hours. A shorter direct 3¾ mile walk (**B**) to Moel Hiraddug is included.
START Prestatyn-Dyserth Way car park [SJ 062793]
DIRECTIONS The small car park adjoins the A5151 where the road dips on the eastern side of Dyserth.

Moel Hirradog's hillfort, overlooking Dyserth, is the most northerly of those on the Clwydian Range. The large fort was enclosed by a single stone rampart above its steep western slopes and up to three walls with ditches on its eastern side, with an outer enclosure at its southern end. An inner enclosure on the summit ridge was probably added later. Sadly the northern part of the fort has been destroyed by limestone quarrying. The fort contained at least 50 round-houses. In the 19thC, part of a 2nd century BC ceremonial shield was found here.

From the car park entrance turn LEFT. As the road begins to rise take a signposted path opposite below water treatment works. Follow the waymarked stiled path along the course of an old railway line to a minor road by Grove Mill Cottage. *In 1884, H D Pochin, a local landowner, at his own expense built, the first ¾ mile of a proposed extension of the Prestatyn–Dyserth railway to Trelawnyd. It was never completed beyond Marion Mill.* Follow the road LEFT past the remains of Grove Mill. On the bend take the Offa's Dyke Path (Marion Cwm) along the stone track ahead to Marion Mill. The fast flowing stream powered several local corn or fulling mills. Turn RIGHT and follow the Offa's Dyke Path (ODP) up and along an enclosed green track, then south through two fields to a road. Follow it along a nearby access track (Tyddyn-y-cyll) and over a stile on the left. (For **Walk B** continue up the track and on the bend go through a gate and follow the waymarked permissive path across two fields past an information board to a stone stile. Just beyond turn right along a good path, soon doing a U-turn left up through gorse to rejoin Walk A at point 5.)

2 Continue through two fields to rejoin the track. Follow it LEFT to nearby Tyddyn-y-cyll then continue along a green track to cross a stone stile on the right. The ODP heads up to another stile, then rises steadily across the open pasture of Marian Ffrith guided by waymark posts and down to the road at the hamlet of Marian Cwm. Turn LEFT then go through a kissing gate opposite the chapel. After another kissing gate, the ODP goes up a large field to a stile near its left-hand corner onto a road. Cross the stile opposite, then follow the path round the edge of the long field up to another road. Turn LEFT.

3 After 20 yards, leave the ODP by taking a signposted path on your right up a track past a wood, shortly bending right past a stile to cross another above a gate. Follow the wood perimeter fence to a stile. Go briefly ahead along a narrow track, then follow a path to a stile above a stone building. Continue between the fence and an old embanked boundary to a stile, then follow the path down through mature mixed woodland. Shortly, turn RIGHT down a wide crosspath. When it bends left keep ahead down a narrow path through trees to a road. Keep ahead, then turn LEFT down another road into Cwm. Go past the Church and the Blue Lion Inn, then take a path signposted to Dyserth on the right. Go up the field to a stile by a wood, then up to another stile. Now climb the initially steep field to a stile – *with the southern end of Moel Hiraddug ahead* – then descend the next field edge to a road. Go through a kissing gate opposite to an information board.

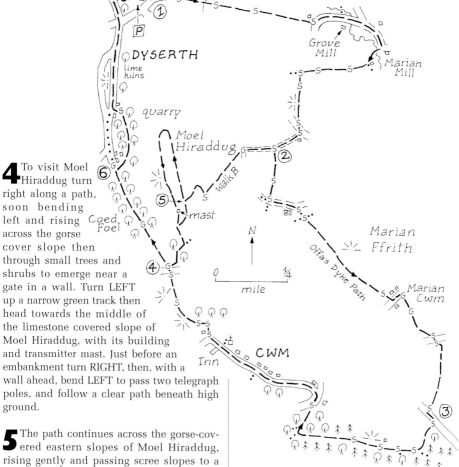

4 To visit Moel Hiraddug turn right along a path, soon bending left and rising across the gorse cover slope then through small trees and shrubs to emerge near a gate in a wall. Turn LEFT up a narrow green track then head towards the middle of the limestone covered slope of Moel Hiraddug, with its building and transmitter mast. Just before an embankment turn RIGHT, then, with a wall ahead, bend LEFT to pass two telegraph poles, and follow a clear path beneath high ground.

5 The path continues across the gorse-covered eastern slopes of Moel Hiraddug, rising gently and passing scree slopes to a fence overlooking the large quarry – *which in the 19thC provided limestone for Mostyn Ironworks and Shotton steelworks.* Now head south up and along the western edge of the grassy ridge – *enjoying superb views* – to its highest point then down to the mast and small building. From the building's left hand side follow a path down to rejoin your outward route by the embankment. (For **Walk B** keep ahead to descend to a gate in a wall corner. Follow a path down through small trees/ shrubs then gorse to an information board by a kissing gate.) From the information board follow a stony path north west beneath Moel Hiraddug, then through Coed Foel down to a finger post at the wood corner just before a seat and viewing board.

6 Either continue ahead along a lane then road through Dyserth, or follow the signposted path, featuring a long flight of steps, across the wooded slope and down to join the road. Follow it past an information board by a lime kiln. At the A5151 go down Pandy Lane opposite. Shortly, go up stone steps on your right and follow a woodland path, soon alongside a stream, then up to the car park.

WALK 3
PENYCLODDIAU

DESCRIPTION This classic 5 mile hill walk (**A**) features Penycloddiau Iron Age hillfort, one of the largest in Wales, a section of Offa's Dyke Path (ODP) and panoramic views. It is one of my favourite walks in all seasons. The route takes the ODP up to the hillfort, then deviates to follows its western ramparts up to Penycloddiau's restored summit cairn (1443 ft/440 metres), where it re-joins the ODP to cross a broad ridge. It then heads south along a spectacular scenic high-level stony track (byway) across Penycloddiau's open western flanks overlooking the Vale of Clwyd, before returning on a path up through Coed Llangwyfan. Allow about 2½ hours. Also included is a 2½ mile walk (**B**) featuring a circuit of the hilfort's impressive ramparts.

START Coed Llangwyfan car park [SJ 139668]

DIRECTIONS From the small roundabout on the B5429 north of Llandyrnog village centre, follow the side road past The Kimnel Arms, then at a cross-roads, turn left signposted Llangwyfan. At a junction, keep ahead, and follow the minor road up the wooded valley for 1 mile to the forestry car park at the top of the pass. Alternatively, from Mold turn off the A541 into Nannerch, then take the first road left for about 3 miles towards Llandyrnog to the car park.

Penycloddiau, meaning 'The hill of the trenches', is one of the largest hillforts in Wales. Its interior, covering some 21 hectares and rising to a summit of 1443 feet/440 metres, is almost ½ mile/800 metres long, enclosed within a single substantial grass-covered rampart, strengthened at its northern end by up to three more. It had entrances on its southern end and midway on its eastern side. There is evidence of level hut platforms. Its restored summit cairn protects a Bronze Age burial site.

I For both walks go past the large gate between information boards into Coed Llangwyfan. Go briefly along the forestry track then follow the ODP up along the forest edge and across an open aspect offering panoramic views. After a stile continue briefly up the southern end of Penycloddiau, then leave the ODP to follow a path angling left to the nearby fence corner. Follow a path by the fence-topped western rampart of the hillfort. After passing a stile the rampart rises in stages – *now with a substantial outer rampart below* – to the summit cairn. (For **Walk B** now follow a path eastwards by the highest rampart, soon descending and bending south across Penycloddiau's steep eastern slopes. After crossing a second narrow green track the path descends then follows the ramparts across the hillside, later bending to rejoin the ODP. Descend to the stile, crossed earlier then about 25 yards below turn RIGHT down through trees to a forestry track. Follow it LEFT across the steep hillside and on down to the start.)

2 Follow the ODP north down to a stile and across a broad green ridge, later descending to a byway beneath Scots pines. Here you leave Offa's Dyke Path and head south on the part stony gated byway along the western slopes of Penycloddiau, past a descending track, a large old water tank and areas of mature woodland. Eventually, just before a gate, take a wide path angling up to a small wooden gate into Coed Llangwyfan and up through the forest to the start.

WALK 4
MOEL ARTHUR

DESCRIPTION A 4 mile undulating walk to Moel Arthur Iron Age hillfort, offering panoramic views. After an initial descent through Coed Llangwyfan the route follows a delightful bridleway up the edge of another wooded valley, then minor road to a bwlch. It then follows the Offa's Dyke Path up to the shoulder of Moel Arthur, diverts to its summit fort, then descends to Coed Llangwyfan. Allow about 2 hours.

START As Walk 3.

The steep conical heather-covered hill of Moel Arthur at 1494 feet/456 metres is crowned by a circular Iron Age hillfort. This small, but prominent, hillfort is defended

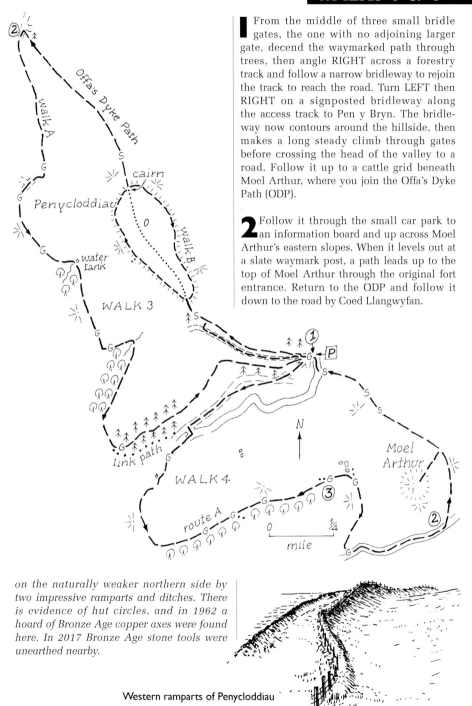

From the middle of three small bridle gates, the one with no adjoining larger gate, decend the waymarked path through trees, then angle RIGHT across a forestry track and follow a narrow bridleway to rejoin the track to reach the road. Turn LEFT then RIGHT on a signposted bridleway along the access track to Pen y Bryn. The bridleway now contours around the hillside, then makes a long steady climb through gates before crossing the head of the valley to a road. Follow it up to a cattle grid beneath Moel Arthur, where you join the Offa's Dyke Path (ODP).

2 Follow it through the small car park to an information board and up across Moel Arthur's eastern slopes. When it levels out at a slate waymark post, a path leads up to the top of Moel Arthur through the original fort entrance. Return to the ODP and follow it down to the road by Coed Llangwyfan.

on the naturally weaker northern side by two impressive ramparts and ditches. There is evidence of hut circles, and in 1962 a hoard of Bronze Age copper axes were found here. In 2017 Bronze Age stone tools were unearthed nearby.

Western ramparts of Penycloddiau

MOEL Y GAER & MOEL FAMAU

DESCRIPTION An undulating 4½ mile walk to visit the Clwydian Range's most remote Iron Age hillfort, then its highest hill and North-East Wales' most iconic landmark, in Moel Famau Country Park, with extensive views throughout. The route first descends upland pasture into a side valley, then makes a short steep climb to the summit of Moel y Gaer hillfort. It then follows a path up across the mainly heather-covered slopes to join the Offa's Dyke Path for a short climb to the top of Moel Famau, with its ruined early 19thC Jubilee Tower. It then returns mainly by Offa's Dyke Path. Allow about 3 hours. For a 3½ mile walk missing out Moel Famau, simply return down the Offa's Dyke Path.

START Car park, Bwlch Penbarras [SJ 162606]

DIRECTIONS From Mold take the A494 towards Ruthin. Shortly after passing Loggerheads Country Park, take a minor road signposted to Moel Famau Country Park/Tafarn-y-Gelyn. Follow this road for 2 miles, past Moel Famau Forest car park & toilets, to reach Bwlch Pen Barras car parks at the top of the pass. Park in the one on the right.

From the northern car park's viewing area overlooking the Vale of Clwyd join the nearby wide stony Offa's Dyke Path. Shortly, at a finger post, go down the signposted path angling LEFT. When it splits ignore the one leading to a stile but continue beside the fence down to a stile/gate below. Follow the path along a faint green track by the fence down the edge of the field – *with a good view of the heather and bracken covered side ridges stretching out like extended fingers, and Moel y Gaer.* Go past a stile and after about 20 yards as the faint slightly sunken track curves left, go through a gap in the low embankment on the right and follow a faint path down the open pasture aiming to cross the end of the right-hand shoulder of the small gorse-capped hill ahead. A clearer path then continues down the hillside to a stile below a waymarked permissive bridleway

gate. Follow the wide path down below the fence.

2 Just before a gate in it do a sharp U-turn RIGHT on the waymarked permissive bridleway towards an attractive side valley below Moel y Gaer. At a waymark post continue ahead with the permissive bridleway along a narrow old green track above a stream, shortly bending left to a confluence of streams at a small quarry. Cross both streams and go up the wide stony path. After a few yards, when it begins to bend left, go up a path ahead past a large rock outcrop then up the steep mainly bracken-covered southern slope of Moel y Gaer. At a tree when the path splits take the left fork to cross the hillfort's rampart just ahead and go up over another. Continue up the slope ahead then follow a path across the interior of the hillfort – *with a view of Jubilee Tower on Moel Famau* – past a small collection of stones at its highest point to pass through ramparts at its north-eastern corner.

3 The clear path continues east, parallel with the fence about 20 yards to your left. Shortly it begins to rise, passing above the fence corner – *with a good view looking back to Moel y Gaer hillfort* – and continues up through heather, with an attractive side valley below. It then bends half-left across a more open slope and continues up across the heather and bilberry hillside. After briefly levelling out it rises again through heather then continues to the nearby hidden Offa's Dyke Path. .

4 Follow it north up to the ruined Jubillee Tower on the summit of Moel Famau. *The tower dating to 1810, was built by public subscription to commemorate George III's 50 years as king. It was designed by Thomas Harrison of Chester and was the first Egyptian-style monument to be built in Britain. It consisted of a rectangular base with four bastions, on which stood an obelisk. Only the base remains, the obelisk having collapsed after storms in 1862. .Specialist stone masons worked in 2013 to reconsolidate parts of the Tower and to reveal the original north-western corner bas-*

tion buried under rubble. The 360 degree views are superb and there are view finding plates to help identify the many places to be seen. The Jubilee Tower is a prominent landmark visible from Cheshire and Merseyside. It remains the focal point for local and national celebrations. Return down the Offa's Dyke Path, which you can follow all the way down to the start. But shortly, for a variation, at a waymark post, take a path angling LEFT to an old gateway in the adjoining wall, with a stile nearby. Continue south along the path

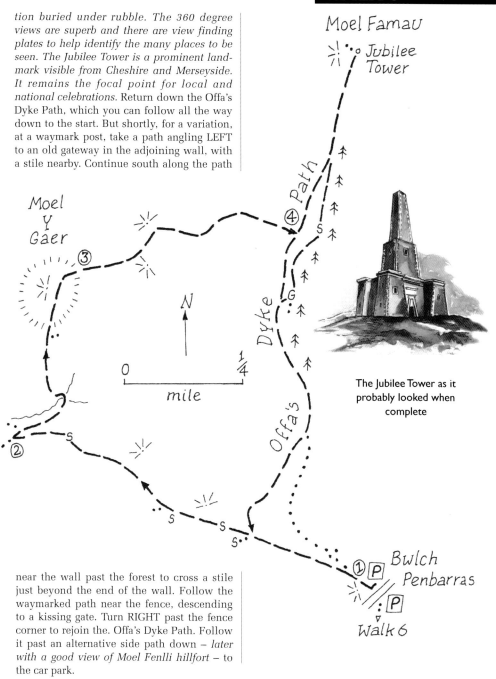

Moel Famau

Jubilee Tower

Moel Y Gaer

N

0   ¼

mile

The Jubilee Tower as it probably looked when complete

Bwlch Penbarras

Walk 6

near the wall past the forest to cross a stile just beyond the end of the wall. Follow the waymarked path near the fence, descending to a kissing gate. Turn RIGHT past the fence corner to rejoin the. Offa's Dyke Path. Follow it past an alternative side path down – *later with a good view of Moel Fenlli hillfort* – to the car park.

WALK 6

MOEL FENLLI

DESCRIPTION A 4 mile walk (**A**) featuring the impressive Iron Age hillfort of Moel Fenlli and extensive views. The walk first visits the hillfort by a choice of routes: a short steep direct climb to Moel Fenlli's summit (**a**) or the Offa's Dyke Path which climbs more steadily across the hillside before contouring round the hillfort's ramparts (**b**). Both routes combine to continue with the Offa's Dyke Path down Moel Fenlli's southern slopes and across fields, before leaving it to follow a delightful high-level bridleway/track across the foothill of Fron Hen and down to join a minor road. A waymarked path takes you through the roadside edge of mixed woodland via Moel Famau Forest car park and picnic site with toilets up to the start. Allow about 2½ hours. Combining both routes (**a**) and (**b**) makes an excellent short 1¼ mile Moel Fenlli walk (**B**).

START Car park at Bwlch Penbarras
[SJ 162605]

DIRECTIONS From Mold take the A494 towards Ruthin. Shortly after passing Loggerheads Country Park, take a minor road signposted to Moel Famau Country Park/Tafarn-y-Gelyn. Follow this road for 2 miles, past Moel Famau Forest car park & toilets, to reach two Bwlch Penbarras car parks at the top of the pass. Park in the one on the left.

Moel Fenlli is an impressive hillfort with a naturally steep southern slope and double ramparts defending the north and east of the hill, with its main entrance on the west side. It is the highest in the Clwydian Range (1676 feet/511 metres) and its interior is extensive, with possible platforms for 61 roundhouses. It also has a possible Bronze Age burial mound on its summit. The fort had a good supply of water from its own spring. In 1816 1,500 Roman coins were found here.

1 **Route (a):** For the climb to the top of the hillfort, go to the far end of the car park to two forestry tracks. Here, take a path ahead up to a kissing gate, then up across the tree-covered slope, soon bending up the hillside to a stile. The path now rises more steeply up the northern heather-covered slope of Moel Fenlli to rejoin the fence, and continues up to pass through the fort's lower ramparts and ditch. It then heads along the next rampart before bending away to reach the small summit cairn for panoramic views. Head south down the path to rejoin the rampart. Here the path, soon stepped, bends right down towards the Vale of Clwyd to join the Offa's Dyke Path at a waymark post at point 2.

Route (b): Just before the car park entrance follow a surfaced path leading left to join the signposted Offa's Dyke Path where it crosses the road. Follow it up and across the northern slopes of Moel Fenlli and into the hillfort through its western entrance. Continue with the delightful path beside the higher of two ramparts, soon bending east and rising to a waymark post at descending stepped route (a) from the summit.

2 Follow the Offa's Dyke Path across Moel Fenlli's southern slope before descending steeply to a stile and another beyond at the corner of a forest. Follow the path to a stile at the other forest corner into a field, then the fence on your right down the large field to a stile by a wood corner. Go along the field edge past the wood and down to a finger post in the corner at a crossroad of bridleways/paths.

3 Here you leave the Offa's Dyke Path by turning LEFT to a stile/gate and going down a green track. At a wood corner bend LEFT up the track beside a wall to gates, then RIGHT up to a set of bridle gates above a farm. Now follow the delightful gated green track/bridleway round the open slopes of Fron Hen, offering excellent changing views: *south over the Clwydian Range to Llandegla Moors, Horseshoe Pass, Llantisilio Mountain and the Berwyns beyond; east to Eryrys mountain; and later, north east to Moel Findeg, Deeside, Merseyside, and, on a clear day, the distant Pennines.* Later, the track begins a steady descent to a gate by a house onto a minor road. Follow it LEFT past Pen-y-Waun to a T-junction.

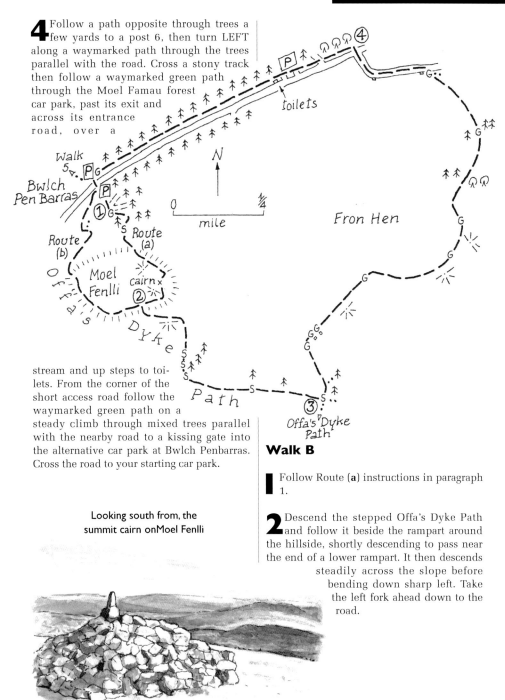

4 Follow a path opposite through trees a few yards to a post 6, then turn LEFT along a waymarked path through the trees parallel with the road. Cross a stony track then follow a waymarked green path through the Moel Famau forest car park, past its exit and across its entrance road, over a

toilets

Walk 5

Bwlch Pen Barras

Route (b)

Route (a)

Moel Fenlli

cairn x

Fron Hen

N

0 — ¼ mile

Dyke

Path

Offa's Dyke Path

stream and up steps to toilets. From the corner of the short access road follow the waymarked green path on a steady climb through mixed trees parallel with the nearby road to a kissing gate into the alternative car park at Bwlch Penbarras. Cross the road to your starting car park.

Looking south from, the summit cairn onMoel Fenlli

Walk B

I Follow Route (a) instructions in paragraph 1.

2 Descend the stepped Offa's Dyke Path and follow it beside the rampart around the hillside, shortly descending to pass near the end of a lower rampart. It then descends steadily across the slope before bending down sharp left. Take the left fork ahead down to the road.

MOEL Y GAER, LLANTISILIO MOUNTAIN

DESCRIPTION An exhilarating 8 mile (**A**) or 7¼ mile (**B**) ridge walk along the highest hills above the Dee Valley, an Open Access area, featuring Moel y Gaer Iron Age hillfort and panoramic views, followed by a contrasting low-level return. This undulating route starts from the top of the Horseshoe Pass (1367 feet/417 metres), so reducing the climbing involved. It first rises to Moel y Faen, from where there are a choice of routes. Walk B continues directly along the wide ridge path up to Moel y Gamelin (1893 feet/577 metres) with its Bronze Age burial cairn, then descends to the bwlch. Walk A follows a delightful less known narrow path to overlook Berwyn slate quarry, then contours across the steep southern mid-slopes of Moel y Gamelin – not suitable for vertigo sufferers – to rejoin the ridge path at the bwlch. The walk continues with the undulating ridge path to Moel y Gaer (1653 feet/504 metres) and Moel Morfydd (1801 ft/549 metres), then returns along the edge of the lush green Morwynion valley. Allow about 4½ hours. A shorter 6 mile walk (**C**) is included.

START The Ponderosa Cafe & Gift Shop, Horseshoe Pass [SJ 193481]

DIRECTIONS From Llangollen take the A542 towards Ruthin and the Horseshoe Pass. At the top of the Pass is an informal off-road parking area opposite the Ponderosa Cafe.

*M*oel y Gaer *hillfort crowns one of the lower heather and bilberry summits of Llantisilio Mountains, a range of open hills running west from the top of the Horseshoe Pass above the Dee Valley. It overlooks an important ancient crossing point in the range between Moel y Gaer and Moel y Gamelin linking the Dee Valley and the Vale of Clwyd, The small hillfort is enclosed by a single rampart with an inturned entrance on the east, and further protected by a ditch on the north side. It contains the remains of hut platforms, indicating occupation, possibly seasonal.*

1 Angle past boulders and go up a way-marked wide stony path. Go past a path on the right and angle RIGHT across a stony track, then follow a wide green path up the heather covered hillside, later passing well to the left of a large quarry. At a fence section bend right along a wide stony path to the topof Moel y Faen. *Here are panoramic all round views: from Snowdonia to Shropshire and from the coast to the Berwyn mountains.* Continue ahead down the main wide stony ridge path.

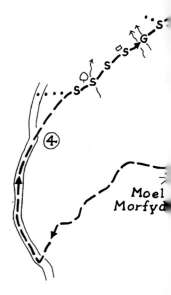

Moel Morfyd

2 Where the path is joined by a fence on the right and before its corner, take a narrow path angling left through heather. (For **Walk B** continue with the ridge path over Moel y Gamelin and down to point 3.) Continue with the clear path across the hillside, shortly gently rising, to reach a good viewpoint overlooking the Horseshoe Pass road and Berwyn Quarry – *one of the few remaining quarries in North Wales* – visible below. *Beneath the buildings can be seen an old incline and the connecting tramway which was used to transport the slate around the hillside down the valley to the Llangollen canal.* The narrow path contours across the steep slope above the quarry road, then gradually descends to cross a stream in a small

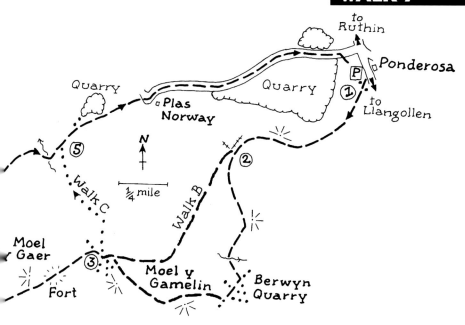

side valley. The path continues south east through bracken then heather and bilberry towards a small peak adjoining the quarry. After about 100-120 yards from the stream, in a flattish area, turn RIGHT along a level narrow side path heading south west, soon passing over a cross path. At a path angling in from the left go half-RIGHT up another path and across the steep hillside above the side valley and on to join the ridge path at the bwlch between Moel y Gamelin and Moel y Gaer.

3 Continue up the wide ridge path to the summit of Moel y Gaer. (For **Walk C** return down to the bwlch then take the second path on the left down an attractive side valley to a boundary wall where you rejoin the main walk at point 5.) The ridge path now descends, before rising up to the trig point on Moel Morfydd. Continue along the ridge, later descending to a road. Turn RIGHT. Shortly the road begins to descend into the Morwynion valley.

4 After about ½ mile, as the road bends down left, take the signposted bridleway ahead across the bilberry/heather/bracken

covered hillside to a stile/gate. Keep ahead on the waymarked path to cross a stile and a stream. Continue with the fence to a stile/gate and on to a further stile/gate above a farm. Keep ahead, soon descending to cross a stream. After a small gate cross another stream and continue ahead to a stile/gate at a signposted bridleway/path junction. Go up the rough track ahead and follow it to a gate. Keep ahead to cross a stream and go through a facing gate, then continue on a delight-ful path, shortly bending down to cross a stream flowing from an attractive side valley. A rougher path rises then continues near a fence to where it joins a wall by a gate.

5 Continue near the wall for about 100 yards, then follow a green track angling away and rising, becoming a path, to cross the right side of a low fence corner above a small quarry. Continue ahead alongside the fence, then across the large field to a low fence onto a road below. Follow the road past nearby Plas Norway and later, quarry spoil heaps. About 100 yards before the main road, take a path angling RIGHT across heather covered ground to the start, and well earned refreshments at the Ponderosa Café.

CASTELL DINAS BRAN

DESCRIPTION This undulating 5¼ mile walk (**A**) climbs to the spectacular hilltop ruin of Castell Dinas Bran (1,050 feet/320 metres) above Llangollen, offering panoramic views, then descends and continues past Llandyn Hall to the Sun Trevor Inn. It returns along a delightful World Heritage Site section of the Llangollen Canal. Allow about 3½ hours. A shorter 2¾ mile walk (**B**) is included.

START Mill Street riverside car park, Llangollen [SJ 216422]

DIRECTIONS The long stay car park lies just off the A539 near the Ponsonby Arms pub.

*C*astell *Dinas Bran, now a romantic ruin, occupies the site of an Iron Age fort on a steep isolated hill overlooking Llangollen. The original hillfort consists of a single rampart and ditch, with an inturned entrance at its south-western corner. There is recent evidence of possible roundhouses. The castle is believed to have been built about 1260 by the Welsh Prince, Gruffydd ap Madoc. By 1277 it had been deliberately abandoned and burned to prevent its use by Edward I's invading army. An English garrison was placed there, and despite its subsequent return to Welsh ownership, the castle was never rebuilt.*

1 Follow the path through Riverside Gardens, soon above the Dee, to steps just before 14thC Llangollen Bridge onto the A539. Cross to the Bridge End Hotel opposite and nearby Riverside Taxidermy, then go up Wharf Hill to cross over the canal at The Wharf. At the junction follow an enclosed path ahead past a school and up to a kissing gate and access lane. Follow the path ahead up to another kissing gate above a house. Go up its access track to a junction of tracks and lane. Go up the track ahead to a kissing gate then up the path angling RIGHT. Continue towards Castell Dinas Bran, then follow a zig-zag path up to the ruined castle. From its eastern end descend the hillside to a gate, then follow a waymarked path down to a kissing gate onto a narrow road.

2 Follow it RIGHT down to Wern-uchaf. (For **Walk B** continue down the road to Llangollen.) Cross a stile on the left, then go along the field edge past the farm to a facing gateway. Go half-LEFT across the next field to a stile. Turn LEFT to a small gate and follow the fence down to gates. Go down the field to a stile onto Llandyn Hall's driveway and cross another stile ahead. Follow a green track up to gates near an outbuilding,

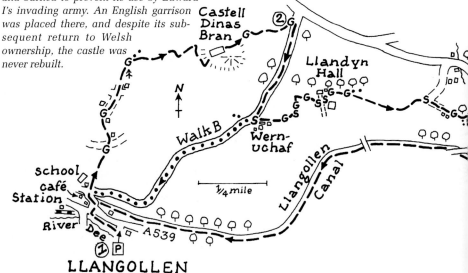

then up to further gates on your right. Follow the waymarked path across the mid-slopes of a large field to a stile in the top boundary onto a lane. Follow it RIGHT down past an old cottage and new house. Go along a short stony track to a gate, briefly down an enclosed path, then turn LEFT down to a footbridge over a stream in a dingle, then a stile. Go across the field to another stile, then head LEFT up to a waymark post. Follow a path RIGHT through an old tree boundary, past a cottage and on to a stile/gate, then up to a road. Go along it.

3 After a cattle grid the road descends. Soon turn sharp RIGHT on the signposted Community Miles Route to Tan y bont. Go down steps then an enclosed path, at a path junction bending right down to Haulfryn's entrance. Just beyond turn RIGHT down the road to the Sun Trevor. Cross the A539 and a bridge over the canal. Follow the canal towpath1¾ miles back to Llangollen Wharf.

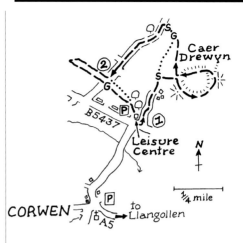

WALK 9

CAER DREWYN

DESCRIPTION A 2½ mile walk from Corwen featuring Caer Drewyn, one of the best preserved Iron Age hillforts in Wales and a former railway cutting. Allow 1½ hours.

START Corwen Leisure Centre [SJ 083441]

DIRECTIONS The Leisure Centre lies on the B5437 just north of Corwen centre.

Caer Drewyn occupies a strategic position overlooking several valley routes. It is a complex site developed over three phases. An early small enclosure was later superseded by this larger fort. Unlike other local hillforts it is not encircled by earthen banks and ditches, but substantial stone ramparts which extend down the slope of the hill. It has inturned entrances on its western side and at its NE corner near its highest point (964 feet/294 metres), which also con-

tains possible guard-chambers. It's interior contains evidence of roundhouses. Tradition has it was later used by Owain Gwynedd and Owain Glyndŵr in their struggles against the English monarchy.

I Turn LEFT along the B5437, then LEFT again on a signposted path to Caer Drewyn up an access lane to a house. Continue up a green track to a stile/gate, then take the signposted path up the hillside. Turn RIGHT up a track, soon following the curve of the fort's ramparts to level out near its north-east corner. Turn LEFT through the fort's entrance to a small cairn marking the highest point. Head west down the fort's expansive interior, close to its northern ramparts, to pass through the lower entrance to rejoin the track. Follow it down to a kissing gate then turn RIGHT along a green track to a stile/gate. Continue along the hedge-lined track, then turn LEFT along another track, later joining an access lane.

2 At Corwen Cutting – *part of the former Denbigh, Ruthin and Corwen Railway (1864-1962)* – turn RIGHT through a squeeze gap and follow the path above the cutting, shortly descending into it, then returning along the other side to the road. Go through the squeeze gap opposite and follow the path down into the cutting then along the former railway embankment to the Leisure Centre.

WALK 10

CAER EUNI

DESCRIPTION A meandering 5½ mile walk (**A**), with extensive views, exploring an attractive upland area of Open Access north-east of Bala, once occupied by early man, It visits two important early historical sites: the impressive Iron-Age hillfort of Caer Euni (1197 feet/365 metres) offering extensive views and Bronze Age circular cairns. The route includes a shorter 3 mile walk (**B**) and can easily be varied to include .Llyn Caer- Euni. Allow about 3½ hours.

START Bethel [SH 988398]

DIRECTIONS Leave Bala on the A494 towards Corwen, and after nearly 5 miles, upon reaching the hamlet of Bethel, turn left on a minor road opposite the B4402 (Llandderfel). A small parking space is immediately on the left.

*B**ethel,** so named after a chapel was built here in the early 19thC, was an important stopping place for drovers. They stayed at The Boot – an inn up to the 1930s – and their cattle were kept in a field opposite. There was a smithy, and at one time a school. The minor road is on the line of the Roman road running east from Caergai to Chester.*

*C**aer Euni** is a long narrow hillfort which overlooked this important ancient valley route. It utilised a steep slope on its south-east side, with ramparts and a ditch on its north-west side, and an entrance at the north-east. It was later enlarged and strengthened to the south-west, with a rock-cut ditch and stonier rampart. The fort contains about 20 possible round house platforms, most in the enlarged area.*

I Walk along the road past the former chapel, and on past Blaen Cwm. About 150 yards further, before another house, do a sharp u-turn LEFT on a signposted path up a rough track back across the young tree-covered slope, soon bending sharp right and rising steadily past side tracks to a stile. Continue ahead near the boundary, in the field corner bending LEFT to a ladder-stile. Follow the old embanked boundary ahead

up to cross another stile. Bear RIGHT to follow a path along slightly higher and drier ground parallel with the nearby fence to join a track. Follow it for about 50 yards, then just before a gate across it, turn LEFT along a path across reedy ground, following the tree/fence boundary on the right to go through a facing gateway in the corner. Follow a path ahead up to cross the ramparts and ditch of Caer Euni hillfort and on to its large summit cairn for all-round views. Return to the gateway, then bear RIGHT along a path near the fence, after a few yards bending LEFT to follow a choice of paths down to join the fence on your right to cross a stile by a gate in it to join a cross-path beyond. (For Walk B follow it left up to the stone circles.)

2 Turn RIGHT down the path and across the field passing to the left of an old stile/fence and continuing to a gate onto a road. Go up the road. At a signposted cross-path, turn LEFT down the access track to Tyn-yr-Erw and cross a stile to the left of the cottage. Turn LEFT along the reedy field edge and through a gate in the corner. Follow the path leading half-RIGHT to a waymark post amongst gorse, then turn RIGHT down through trees, over a stream, and past another waymark post to a ladder-stile. Go down the field to a stile in the right-hand corner and down the next field edge to cross another stile. Turn LEFT and cross a nearby moss covered wall. Now follow a path, guided by a series of waymark posts down through the wood to a stony track at its corner near a short gated walled section. (If you emerge from the wood lower down follow the track left.)

3 Go through the gate opposite, then turn LEFT up the field edge, through an old gateway and on down the next field edge – *with the attractive wooded valley of Cwm Main, once occupied by Quakers, ahead* – to cross a stile on the left. Go across tussocky ground and through trees to reach a green track leading from a nearby small corrugated shed. Follow it RIGHT, soon fading, then continue ahead on a waymarked path alongside the fence of a game-bird rearing area to a stile. The path continues along the bot-

16

tom edge of attractive woodland, shortly rising to a gateway, then across the more open slope to a gate onto an access track. About 15 yards beyond a cattle-grid, as the track descends towards restored Tyddyn Tyfod – *once occupied by Edward ap Rhys, who went with the first group of Welsh Quakers to Pennsylvania in 1682* – turn LEFT on a waymarked path up between the fence and a tree boundary to a stile. Continue up the enclosed path across the hillside.

4 At the top turn LEFT through a gate just before a stile (a link path to Llyn Caer-Euni). Turn LEFT and follow a path along the moorland edge, over a stream at the top of a gully, then towards a solitary large tree ahead. Just before it go up the slope ahead to the highest point for all-round views (or continue past the tree, taking the path's right fork beneath the craggy slopes) then descend south. At the bottom of the slope turn LEFT to a stile in the fence. Keep ahead, then just before a boundary corner, turn RIGHT to the other boundary corner. Continue ahead up and across short tussocky ground to a clear cross path. Follow it RIGHT to the remains of Cefn Caer-Euni bronze age stone circles at a good viewpoint. *The large kerb circle and a smaller ring cairn were used for ceremonial and burial purposes. The larger circle was said to have been used as a cockpit in the 18thC when cockfighting was popular in the area.*

5 Continue along the path to a small gate, then head slightly LEFT on a path across the broad moorland ridge to go through the right of two gates. Turn LEFT and immediately before the other gate turn RIGHT along an improving path/ old reedy track – *soon with a view of Llyn Caer-Euni nestling below* – passing close to the small ridge on the left to cross a stile beyond its end. Turn LEFT and follow the old then new fence down to a stile/gate near the wood corner. Follow a path ahead down below the fence, then do a sharp u-turn RIGHT down an old reedy track to a waymarked gateway and old stile. Now go down the left-hand edge of the old part tree-lined sunken track and past the side of a house to the road by the start.

17

WALK 11
CAER CARADOG

DESCRIPTION A 6 mile walk (**A**) exploring a little visited area of interesting attractive countryside, offering extensive views and passing close to the small isolated hillfort of Caer Caradog. The route heads west from Cwm Alwen and visits a small hidden attractive reservoir. Later it rises, initially on an old green track, across upland pasture to pass the hillfort. It then follows the waymarked Hiraethog Trail, first along a delightful old drovers' road across upland pasture beneath Mwdwl-eithin, then down to Llanfihangel, with its old drovers' inn and ancient church to visit. Allow about 3½ hours.
START Llanfihangel Glyn Myfyr [SH 987496]
DIRECTIONS From Cerrigydrudion, take the B5105 towards Ruthin, and after descending the steep hill into Llanfihangel, turn left along a road just before the bridge and the Crown Inn. Follow it past the church to riverside picnic parking areas.

L *Llanfihangel Glyn Myfyr was the birthplace of Owain Myfyr (Owen Jones) in 1741, a successful London businessman with an interest in old Welsh manuscripts. He was an important patron of Welsh literary works, including the publication of the 'Myfyrian Archaiology of Wales'. The poet William Wordsworth stayed here in 1824 and was inspired to write a poem about the area.*
C *aer Caradog Iron Age hillfort is situated at about 1246 feet/380 metres on a spur overlooking Cerrigydrudion and important valley routes. It has a large rampart and ditch, with an entrance on its eastern side.*

I From the furthest picnic area by an adventure play area just before the former school take a signposted path through a gate on the left. Follow a rising stony track above a stream. After a gate take the main track bearing RIGHT to go through a gate over the stream. Go half-LEFT up the field to rejoin the track and follow it to gates, past a stone barn to another gate. Continue up the green track past the old farmhouse. As it bends left across the stream continue ahead briefly along its left-hand bank, then up the field edge by an old reedy sunken track to a gap in its corner. Follow the green track ahead for 10 yards, and go through a gap on the left in the gorse-covered boundary. Continue along the right-hand field edge by the old reedy track towards a wind turbine, then in the corner bend LEFT up to a waymarked gate in the top corner. Go through a gap in the old wall just ahead, and follow the boundary on your left up to go through a waymarked gate in it, near the corner.

2 Go through the waymarked gate just above. Head west (waymark misleading) across upland pasture to a waymarked gate just before ruined buildings by a rocky escarpment. Go past the old outbuilding and through a gate on the right just beyond the ruined cottage. Angle LEFT to the boundary and go down the field edge to see the hidden small attractive rowan tree edged part lily-covered reservoir – *home for wildfowl and a quiet spot for fishing.* Retrace your steps, and after passing through the gate by the cottage, go half-RIGHT and through a waymarked gate. Go half-LEFT to another waymarked gate. Turn RIGHT along the next field edge to a gate by a nearby house and down its access track to a gate. Turn LEFT along a lane past Maes Tyddyn farm, and on to reach the B5105. Turn RIGHT down the grass verge.

3 Shortly, take a signposted path through the farmyard of Tyn y Mynydd opposite to cross a stream and a stile beyond. Follow an old green track up to a gate, then up across the open western slopes of Y Drum – *offering excellent views west towards Cerrigydrudion and the mountains of Snowdonia beyond.* After passing a short section of collapsed wall, go through a gate ahead. Continue up by the fence to a gate in its corner at its highest point. Continue beside the fence, with the distinctive ramparts of Caer Caradog hillfort to your right. The fence descends to a gate. Go past the fence corner ahead and down the field to a ladder-stile onto a minor road. Follow it LEFT and at a junction, keep ahead to pass

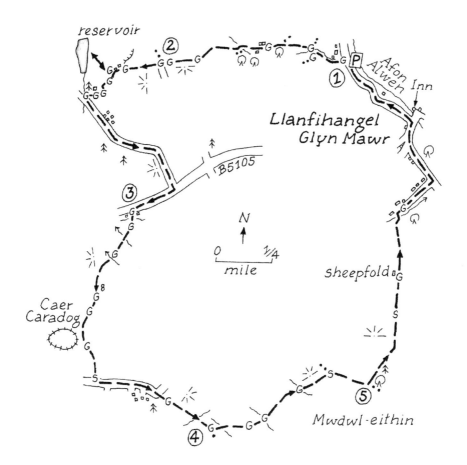

two farms. When the road bends left, go along a green track ahead to a gate. Continue along this delightful enclosed old drovers route to a gate into open country, where you join the Hiraethog Trail.

4 Continue with the green track near the wall rising steadily up the hillside, passing through two gates. After another it continues along the edge of upland pasture and the heather-covered slopes of Mwdwl-eithin to a stile/gate. Continue along the green track – *enjoying the extensive views.*

5 Just before the next gate on the track, the waymarked Hiraethog Trail bends LEFT and follows another green track on a long steady descent towards Llanfihangel, to a ladder-stile/gate, then a gate by a sheepfold. Now follow an old gorse lined green track down the hillside to a gate. Go ahead down the next field edge to join a stony track, which bends down towards a farm. Cross the nearby footbridge over the stream to a small gate beneath the barn. Go through the gate ahead and along the old farm's driveway. At a junction, turn LEFT along the road into Llanfihangel. At the next junction, turn RIGHT to reach the B5105. Cross the road and follow it down to the junction. If not tempted by the nearby Crown Inn – *a traditional pub with a scenic beer garden above the river* – turn LEFT along the road past 13thC St Michael's church back to the start.

MYNYDD Y GAER

DESCRIPTION A choice of 2 mile (**A**), 1½ mile (**B**) or 1¼ mile (**C**) walks featuring the easily accessible ancient hillfort of Mynydd y Gaer (918 feet/ 280 metres), offering panoramic views. After passing round its western ramparts Walk A returns along its lower slopes past Plas - uchaf reservoir. Walk B returns via its north eastern side, whilst Walk C explores the hillfort's interior. Allow about 1½ hours.

START Parking area 1 mile west of Llannefydd [SH 973711]

DIRECTIONS From Llannefydd follow the road west out of the village. Go past a road on the left, then take a road angling right to find a large parking area on the left.

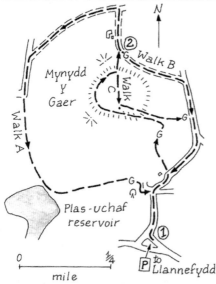

Mynydd y Gaer hillfort, possibly Iron Age or later, stands on a small hill dominating the landscape just NW of Llannefydd. It was originally enclosed by an outer bank, ditch and stone rampart, the remains of which are most evident on its western side. It has a staggered entrance on its northern side.

At the nearby junction bend RIGHT up the road. On the bend take the higher of the two roads up to Bron Hwylfa and a signposted path on the left. The wide path rises steadily, then narrows to reach a small gate. The path soon bends up across the southern slopes of Mynydd y Gaer. After passing a path on the right near its summit continue beside the remains of the hillfort's ramparts, soon bending north across the very steep western slopes. The path then begins a steady descent to reach a narrow green track coming down from the hillfort's centre. (For **Walk C** turn right up the track to level out at a path junction near the fort's summit and your outward route. Turn left along a wide path past the nearby fence corner and eastwards beside the fence to a gate to join the road beyond. Follow it right down to Bron Hwylfa.) Follow the track down to a stony track. (For **Walk B** turn right to the nearby gate/cattle grid and follow the track to join the narrow road left earlier. Follow it down to Bron Hwylfa.)

2 For **Walk A** follow the stony track down past Ty-newydd, then bend LEFT down its stony access track to a road. Follow it LEFT, then on the bend go along an initially wide path ahead beneath Mynydd y Gaer's steep slopes, shortly passing Plas-uchaf reservoir – _built in 1870_. The path continues beneath Mynydd y Gaer's southern slopes to a small gate. Follow the main path up through trees to the bend of the road and your outward route.

CASTELL CAWR

DESCRIPTION A meandering 2½ mile Woodland Trust circular walk through Coed y Gopa, a prominent wooded limestone hill overlooking Abergele to the hidden impressive Castell Cawr hillfort, returning by another notable feature, Ffos y Bleiddiaid (Ditch of the Wolves). A gem of a walk, waymarked in key places, through attractive ancient woodland, large parts of which were replanted in the 1950s. Allow about 1½ hours.

START Coed y Gopa main entrance, Abergele [SH 934772]

DIRECTIONS Follow the A547 west through Abergele and across the roundabout by Tesco's. At the entrance to Gwyrch Castle turn left along Ffordd Tan'r Allt, then right up Tan-y-Gopa past the Golf Club. At the junction by a path entrance to Coed y Gopa (an alternative start) continue up the road past the council depot to a small limestone car parking area opposite Gwyrch Castle Lodge.

*C*astell Cawr *(Giant's Castle) stands on the summit of Coed y Gopa (620 feet/ 189 metres) With sheer cliffs to the north-east and massive earth ramparts elsewhere this small well-defended hillfort, prior to the growth of woodland, was in a commanding location overlooking the lower Clwyd valley and coast. It contains the remains of several roundhouse platforms.*

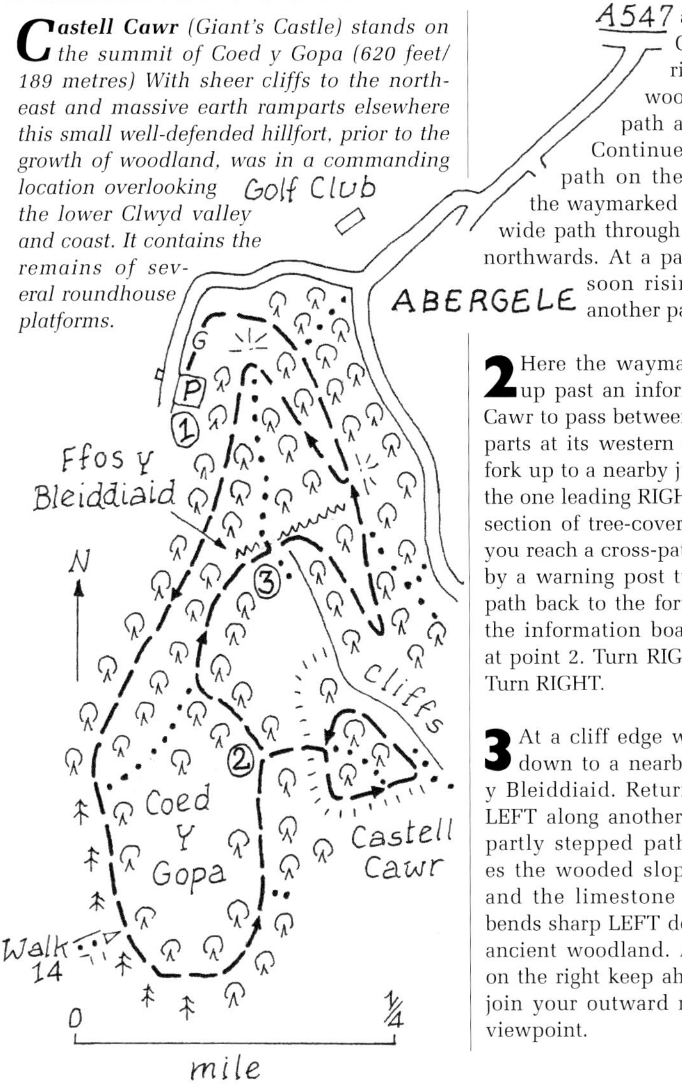

*F*fos y Bleiddiaid *is a deep narrow cleft mined for lead and copper, possibly since Roman times, and now an important habitat for bats.*

Go up to an information board and kissing gate into Coed y Gopa. Go up the stony track past a stepped path from the alternative start to reach a bench seat at a great viewpoint. Here bend sharp RIGHT up the track. Soon it bends left opposite a mound offering extensive coastal views, including Gwyrch Castle. The track rises steadily through the wood, later joined by a wide path angling in from the left. Continue along the track past a path on the right to its end. Here the waymarked trail turns LEFT along a wide path through the trees, soon bending northwards. At a path junction keep ahead, soon rising, then descending to another path junction.

2 Here the waymarked trail turns RIGHT up past an information board on Castell Cawr to pass between the massive earth ramparts at its western entrance. Take the right fork up to a nearby junction of paths. Follow the one leading RIGHT round to pass another section of tree-covered ramparts. Just before you reach a cross-path on the top of the cliffs by a warning post turn LEFT along another path back to the fort's entrance. Return past the information board to the path junction at point 2. Turn RIGHT to a path T-junction. Turn RIGHT.

3 At a cliff edge warning post bend LEFT down to a nearby footbridge across Ffos y Bleiddiaid. Return a few yards and turn LEFT along another path by the fence. The partly stepped path descends, then crosses the wooded slope beneath a high fence and the limestone escarpment. Shortly it bends sharp LEFT down through a section of ancient woodland. At a path angling down on the right keep ahead, soon descending to join your outward route at the bench seat/ viewpoint.

[Map annotations: A547, Golf Club, ABERGELE, Ffos y Bleiddiaid, N, Coed Y Gopa, Castell Cawr, Cliffs, Walk 14, G, P, ①, ②, ③, 0, ¼, mile]

21

PEN-Y-CORDDYN-MAWR

DESCRIPTION A 7 mile walk of great variety exploring the coast and unspoilt rural hinterland between Abergele and Llanddulas, featuring two hillforts sites and good views. The route starts with a 2¼ mile section of the Wales Coast Path(WCP) to Llanddulas, then heads inland up the hidden attractive Dulas valley. It passes beneath Pen-y-corddyn-mawr, with an option to visit its hillfort. It then heads across fields to Gopa Wood, an attractive wooded hill managed by the Woodland Trust, with an opportunity to visit to hidden Castell Cawr fort (See Walk 13). Allow about 4 hours.

START Pensarn beach [SH 942786]

DIRECTIONS From Pensarn on the A548 coast road go over the railway by the station, and follow it to the third car park by the promenade just beyond the Beach Café.

Pen-y-corddyn-mawr hillfort stands on a impressive limestone hill overlooking the Dulas valley, an Open Access area, about a mile south of Llanddulas, and near the Roman road to Caerhun in the Conwy valley. The large fort's defences consist of natural steep cliffs on three sides and two stone ramparts and ditches on its northern side. Although dating from early Iron Age the finding of various Roman artefacts indicates its use extended into the Roman period, with speculation that it may have been the site of a Roman healing shrine.

I Walk west along the promenade then join the nearby coastal cycle/walkway. (For an alternative initial section follow a stony path above Pensarn's pebble beach.) *Inland, amongst the densely wooded hillside, stands the picturesque but sadly ruined Gwrych Castle. The gothic castellated mansion, with its towers and walls, was built in 1819-22 for Lloyd Bamford Hesketh. The WCP then runs close by the shoreline, passes the Tides café bistro and caravan park, then Llanddulas honeycomb worm reef – a rare and newly formed coastal feature visible at low tide. It*

joins the Afon Dulas where it enters the sea, soon crossing a bridge over the river.

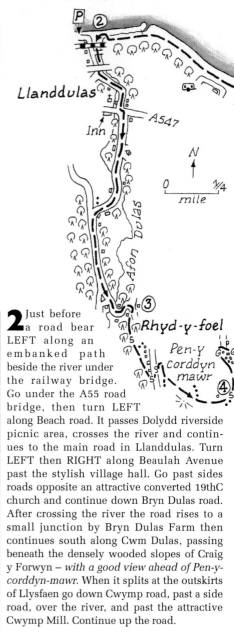

2 Just before a road bear LEFT along an embanked path beside the river under the railway bridge. Go under the A55 road bridge, then turn LEFT along Beach road. It passes Dolydd riverside picnic area, crosses the river and continues to the main road in Llanddulas. Turn LEFT then RIGHT along Beaulah Avenue past the stylish village hall. Go past sides roads opposite an attractive converted 19thC church and continue down Bryn Dulas road. After crossing the river the road rises to a small junction by Bryn Dulas Farm then continues south along Cwm Dulas, passing beneath the densely wooded slopes of Craig y Forwyn – *with a good view ahead of Pen-y-corddyn-mawr.* When it splits at the outskirts of Llysfaen go down Cwymp road, past a side road, over the river, and past the attractive Cwymp Mill. Continue up the road.

3 On the next bend, turn RIGHT on the signposted path along an access track to the gated entrance to Country View. The delightful path continues through trees to a stile, then rises across the wooded slope, shortly passing beneath houses to a kissing gate onto a road beyond at Rhyd-y-foel.

Pensarn Beach

caravan park

toilets

P café

station to A548 Rhyl

A55

Park

A547

ABERGELE

Golf Club

Castell Cawr

Gopa Wood

Betws Lodge Wood

Turn LEFT, then cross a stile on the right opposite Shire Cottage. Follow the meandering path up through the wood to emerge from the trees by the fence beneath Pen-y-corddyn-mawr's impressive limestone crags. From here a path rises across the slope. After about 40 yards go up its left fork to join a wider path just above, which rises steadily across the gorse-covered scree slopes – *enjoying a good view across the valley to the limestone*

escarpment of Craig y Forwyn (Maiden's Leap) and the mountains of Snowdonia. After levelling out the path continues along the left-hand edge of an area of gorse to join the fence descending from Pen-y-corddyn-mawr. Just before its corner the fence is low enough to allow access to the hill's south-western slopes to visit the hillfort, with a small pile of stones at its highest point. Then at the fence corner go through a gap in the old tree boundary and follow a path through the narrow field to cross the old boundary at its end by a small ruin. Descend the slope to another path below. Follow it down to a stile and old gate.

4 Continue down the path then near the fence on your right beneath Pen-y-corddyn-mawr's wooded slope to pass behind houses to a stile/gate by an out-

building onto the driveway below. Turn RIGHT towards Garth Gogof then LEFT across the yard and through a gate at the end of an outbuilding. Follow the stiled path through three fields, then half-RIGHT down the next to a lane. Cross the stile opposite and go along the field edge to gates, then up to the corner of Betws Lodge Wood. Follow the gated track along the edge of two fields past the wood to a large barn. Angle LEFT to a gate and follow a track past Tyddyn-uchaf farm, then another track ahead.

5 On its bend cross a stile ahead into Gopa Wood. Go up the path to a green track, and follow it LEFT, then take an initially wide path angling RIGHT through the trees. Soon divert RIGHT along a side path to the impressive ramparts of Castell Cawr hill-fort (See Walk 13 map). Return to continue north through the wood. At a cliff edge warning post the path bends down to cross a nearby footbridge over Ffos y Bleiddiaid – *a deep narrow cleft mined for lead and copper, possibly since Roman times.* The path continues through the wood, soon descending steadily to a track. (*For a splendid viewpoint turn left to the nearby bend.*) Turn RIGHT down the track, soon doing a sharp U-turn at a good viewpoint. Just before it bends left, descend a long stepped path on your right to a road junction on the edge of Abergele. Go down Tan-y-Gopa road, past the golf club, then turn LEFT along Ffordd Tan'r Allt to the A547 by the entrance to Gwrych Castle. Follow it RIGHT towards Abergele centre, then cross it to go along Sea Road opposite, shortly passing the park and crossing the A55 and railway line to reach the start.

BRYN EURYN

DESCRIPTION A 1 mile waymarked Summit Trail exploring Bryn Euryn, a small part wooded limestone hill overlooking Rhos-on-Sea, now a Local Nature Reserve. The trail passes the ruins of 15thC Llys Euryn and rises to the ancient hill-fort on its open summit (430 feet/131 metres), offering panoramic views. Allow about 1½ hours.

START Bryn Euryn car park, Rhos-on-Sea [SH 834802]

DIRECTIONS The entrance lies at the western end of Rhos road.

*O*n Bryn Euryn's lower slopes are the remains of Llys Euryn – a 15thC fortified mansion, reputedly on the site of an earlier 13thC house owned by Ednyfed Fychan, chief advisor to Llewellyn the Great. Nearby is an old limestone quarry which opened in the 1840s. From here stone was taken by horse drawn railway down Rhos Road to a seafront jetty for shipping by boat. The small Iron Age hillfort is enclosed by cliffs on the south and east sides and by earthen ramparts elsewhere. Unusually it contains a small stronger inner walled defensive area on its rocky summit, dating to the 5thC. It is said to have been the stronghold of Cuneglasus, King of Rhos. Also on its summit are the remains of a World War II radar station.

From the car park entrance follow the waymarked trail along the pavement, then up steps and on to the ruins of Llys Euryn, then up the edge of woodland to Llys Euryn Cottage. Continue ahead along the wide stony path to where the trails split. Follow the Summit Trail up through the wood, soon levelling out. At a crossroad of paths turn LEFT up through the trees then open hillside

past seats to the trig point and information board on the top of Bryn Euryn. Follow the waymarked trail down the steep hillside towards the Little Orme and through trees to join your outward route. Return down the path to go through the kissing gate by Llys Euryn Cottage, then follow a choice of way-marked paths down to the car park.

PEN DINAS

DESCRIPTION A 3 mile undulating walk exploring part of the Great Orme's interesting upland area, offering extensive views. From the summit the walk descends in stages to pass the Ski Centre to visit Pen Dinas Iron Age hillfort. It then returns by an ancient well and 12thC St Tudno's church. Allow about 2 hours.

START Great Orme summit. Llandudno [SH 766853]

DIRECTIONS The summit can be reached by car, no. 73 bus, cable car and tram.

*T*he Summit Complex, built as a hotel in 1903, is the terminus of Britain's most spectacular funicular tramway, which has operated since 1902, as well as Britain's lon-

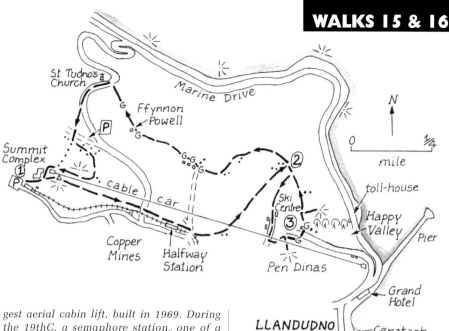

gest aerial cabin lift, built in 1969. During the 19thC, a semaphore station, one of a chain built by Liverpool Dock Trustees, operated here, transmitting messages between Holyhead and Liverpool. A Visitor Centre is nearby.

Pen Dinas fort stands on a spur of the Great Orme overlooking Llandudno, close to Bronze Age copper mines. It has natural steep slopes on three sides and an inner wall and three outer banks on its north-west side. It contains platforms of over 60 roundhouses. Within it is a 'Rocking Stone' (Maen Sigl) reputed to have been used by druids in dealing with people accused of certain misdemeanours. The person stood on the stone, and only if it rocked, was he/she declared innocent! .

1 Head past the Summit Complex up to a trig point for great views. Now .follow a path down to join the tram line, passing close behind the Half-Way station to a stony access track near the bend of the road. Go up the stony track ahead past a barrier to a cable car pillar. Continue on the wide path to a finger post at a junction of paths.

2 Go ahead for a few yards and turn RIGHT down a stepped path, then take its right fork down the edge of the toboggan run and dry ski slope, and a track past the Alpine Lodge. Go down the road then at the car park entrance join a path. Go up its right fork to the summit of Pen Dinas, then return to follow the other path down past a gate by a cattle grid to another gate below. Cross the road and go past a stone shelter at the top of Happy Valley Gardens, then turn LEFT up steps to a gate.

3 Go up the path with the toboggan run and dry ski slope nearby. Soon take a path on the right up to a superb viewpoint. Afterwards continue up the stepped path to the finger post at point 2. Follow the path ahead signposted to 'St. Tudno's church' – with the church soon in view. The way-marked gated 'Summit Trail' path continues past a farm, then Ffynnon Powell to the road by St Tudno's church – named after Tudno, a 6thC Christian who built the first church in the area. Continue up the road, then take the Summit path across open ground and over a stony track. At the next crossroad of paths turn LEFT over crosspaths, then follow the waymarked path up to the Summit Complex.

WALK 17
CAER SEION

DESCRIPTION A delightful 3¾ mile (**A**) or 3 mile (**B**) walk exploring Conwy Mountain, offering panoramic views. The outward route provides an optional additional ½ mile extension to visit a former quarry, before climbing onto its rocky ridge (800 feet/244 metres) containing Caer Seion Iron Age hillfort. It then descends the superb ridge towards Conwy, before returning on the waymarked North Wales Path/Wales Coast Path. Allow about 3 hours.

START Top of Sychnant Pass [SH 750770]

DIRECTIONS Follow the one way system west through Conwy past the railway station. After passing under the town walls, turn left up Mount Pleasant. At the T- junction turn right. Follow the road past the youth hostel for about 1½ miles.

*C*aer Seion *stands on the top of Conwy Mountain overlooking the coast near an important ancient trackway. The original large fort, dating from at least 300 BC, was defended by a single stone rampart and the natural steep slope on its northern side, with an entrance on its south side. Unusually, at a later stage a smaller much stronger fort was built within its western end, with wider walls and ditches, but with no access between the two. There were over 50 roundhouses within the fort. Among interesting items found were a large hoard of sling stones. There is no evidence it was used by the Romans after their conquest of North Wales in 78 AD.*

1 Take the signposted North Wales Path (NWP) down a rough lane passing beneath crags at the head of an impressive valley. It is joined by the Wales Coast Path (WCP) and rises, then continues as a stony track. Shortly it bends left to a finger post. Here turn RIGHT with the NWP through a nearby gate and go up the stony track ahead, shortly descending to a crossroad of narrow tracks by a waymark post. Keep ahead with the NWP/WCP to another waymark post – *with a great view ahead over the quarried hillside to Llandudno and the Great Orme.* (For the quarry extension follow the path ahead down and across the bracken slope onto the wide grass shelf, then return.)

2 Bear RIGHT up the NWP/WCP, then at another post where the NWP/WCP bears right, keep ahead up the stony path, then at a crossroad of paths angle LEFT up the stony path to another path junction. Turn LEFT along the wide path, soon rising, then go up its stonier left fork on to Conwy Mountain. Soon take the path's right fork up onto the small ridge ahead to pass through Caer Seion hillfort with its stone entrance visible below. Shortly the ridge path makes a rocky descent. (An adjoining lower path on the left is an easier option.) *There is a great view down to Conwy with its impressive late 13thC castle.* The main path then levels out before descending again beneath high ground and bending down to the end of a nearby

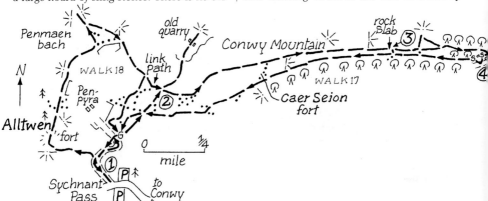

south-facing large rock slab – *with a good view along the Conwy Valley.* (For **Walk B** go to a NWP/WCP waymark post just below to join the returning route at point 4.)

3 Take a wide path continuing east along the ridge, soon descending steadily. At a crossroad of paths continue down the path or better turn LEFT along a small ridge to a metal post overlooking the coast. Turn around and take a path angling LEFT down and across the slope, rising to rejoin the ridge path. Continue down the path, soon by a woodland boundary. At the wall corner the path bends down and round to a ladder-stile above a house, then descends to a road. Follow it RIGHT. Take the signposted NWP/WCP up a driveway to a stile. The path rises steadily to a waymark post at a crossroad of paths by the rock slab met earlier.

4 Follow the NWP/WCP beneath the rock slab then on a long steady climb across the southern slopes of Conwy Mountain, later passing an information board on Caer Seion. Soon after a bench seat the path makes a short descent and splits at a waymark post. Here you leave the NWP/WCP by descending the left fork to join the stony track near the wall below. Follow it to your outward route at the crossroad of tracks. Keep ahead, then take the narrow green left fork up through gorse, then bend LEFT along a wider track down to the gate on your outward route. At the stony access track beyond take the sign-posted NWP over the rise opposite and down to rejoin the track. Follow it back to the start.

WALK 18
DINAS ALLTWEN

DESCRIPTION An enjoyable 2 mile walk exploring an attractive heather covered Open Access area adjoining Conwy Mountain, featuring an early Iron Age hillfort, and panoramic views. Allow about 1½ hours. It can easily be linked to Walk 17 to make a great 4¾ mile circuit.
START Top of Sychnant Pass [SH 750770] See Walk 1.

D inas Alltwen, in contrast to the larger nearby Caer Seion, is a small simple early Iron Age hillfort defended by a single rampart reinforced by a ditch on its north side.

I Take the signposted North Wales Path (NWP) down a rough lane passing beneath crags at the head of an impressive valley. It is joined by the Wales Coast Path (WCP) and rises, then continues as a stony track. At a waymark post opposite a wall corner take a stony path up the heather-covered slope of Alltwen to its summit. Follow a path down its northern side towards a lower top, soon angling RIGHT down to cross the single heather-covered ramparts which enclosed the hillfort. The path now descends more steeply through heather then gorse to a crossroad of paths in a dip. Follow the path ahead and just beyond a small post take its left fork up to a small rise. Follow the path across the hillside, soon descending and continuing past a wall. Follow the path ahead towards Penmaen-bach soon rising beneath a small crag to reach a wall corner. Take a path on the left up Penmaen-bach to a stone cairn on a ridge overlooking the coast. Retrace your steps briefly then take another path leading LEFT up over nearby high ground to the hill's small rocky top. Follow the path down to the wall corner. Go ahead alongside the wall then up the green track, soon levelling out then descending.

2 The track then bends right. (To link with Walk 17 angle left down a path to a cross-path below. Follow it left to join the North Wales Path at a nearby waymark post at point 2 of Walk 17) Follow the track down to a crossroad of paths/tracks. Here follow the track RIGHT towards Alltwen, then take its left fork, over a cross-track, soon bending right and descending. Just before a gate by sheepfolds and the entrance to Pen Pyra turn LEFT to follow the fence to a gate to reach the stony access track beyond. Follow it back to the start.

WALK 19

CAER BACH

DESCRIPTION A 6½ mile (**A**) or 5½ mile (**B**) walk exploring a fascinating scenic upland landscape on the western side of the Conwy Valley beneath Tryfan, full of antiquity, including pre-historic Caer Bach hillfort, and offering panoramic views. The route first rises to the remote ancient St Celynin's church lying at a height of about 920 feet/280 metres. Shortly afterwards there are a choice of routes to Caer Bach. Whilst Walk B heads south directly to the fort Walk A first visits the impressive ancient standing stone of Maen Penddu (about 1345 feet/410 metres) before descending to join Walk B near the fort. The return down to Rowen follows a section of Roman road past standing stones and an ancient burial chamber. Allow about 4 hours.
START Rowen [SH 761719]
DIRECTIONS Rowen is signposted from the B5106. There is roadside parking near the first houses.

R owen, one of the prettiest villages in the Conwy Valley lies on an ancient trackway rising west from the river Conwy through the hills, later used by Romans then drovers. It once had several mills and inns, but only the Ty Gwyn remains.

C aer Bach hillfort stands on the lower eastern slopes of Tal y Fan at about 1355 feet/413 metres. Despite its limited natural defensive position this small fort had strong defences: a massive inner wall encircled by an unusual stone facing outer bank and ditch. It contained a possible roundhouse. The fort's location may relate to the ancient trackway. Its precise age is uncertain but the site was later used in the Medieval period.

▌ Walk through the village past the Ty Gwyn Hotel, attractive stone houses and a chapel. On the bend turn RIGHT on a signposted path along a lane to a farm. Go through the gate ahead, down the field to the bottom left-hand corner to cross a lad-der-stile beyond. Turn RIGHT along a stony track and on the bend cross a ladder-stile ahead. Go along the field edge to another ladder-stile, then follow the raised path up alongside a fence to a narrow road. Follow it RIGHT, then take a signposted path up an access lane on the left past Lwynonn.

2 Later as bends right to a farm cross a lad-der-stile ahead. Go along the right-hand bank of the stream, then cross it and follow the wall on your left up to a waymarked gate in it. Turn RIGHT over the stream then head across to Dodre'r coed cottage. At its entrance turn LEFT up a track, soon bearing RIGHT to a gate above the cottage. The track now rises steadily up the open, then part-wooded hillside. After a small stream, the track bends left then right. About 70 yards further, follow a waymarked path angling RIGHT to cross a nearby ladder-stile/stream and up the tree-covered slope into a field. Continue up to a gate between an outbuilding and a ruined cottage. Pass behind the ruin and go up a path.

3 After about 10 yards, the route turns sharp LEFT past a hawthorn tree. (First follow the wide path ahead to a nearby superb viewpoint.) Follow the improving path up beneath bracken and gorse, then beside a wall up to a ladder-stile. Go along the left-hand side of the small ridge ahead, then across a reedy area, and past another small ridge, with a ruin to your left. Continue along the field, with St. Celynin's church now visible, to a ladder-stile in the top left-hand corner. Go along a green track, then at a track junction turn RIGHT to the church entrance. *Occasional services are still held in this delightful simple Grade 1 listed building, whose nave dates from the 14thC. In the south corner of the churchyard is a rectangular well, renowned for its power to heal sick children. Near the churchyard gate once stood an inn which served travellers crossing the mountains.* Return along the track and past a ladder-stile. When it bends right go through a gate ahead and follow a narrow green track up past a nearby house – *soon with a view of Tal-y-fan ahead* – to a gate into Open Access land by sheepfolds.

28

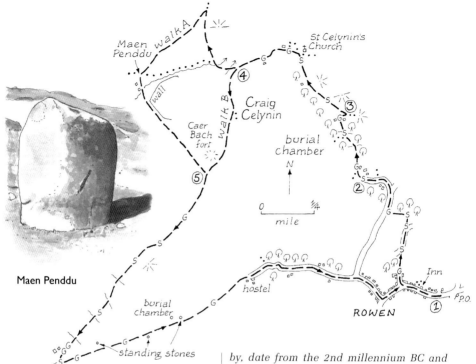

Maen Penddu

standing stones

burial chamber

hostel

ROWEN

Inn

P.O.

Craig Celynin

Caer Bach fort

Maen Penddu

St Celynin's Church

burial chamber

N

0   ¼
mile

walk A

walk B

Go through another gate ahead and follow the green track across open country.

4 After about 150 yards as the track rises half-left you have a choice.

For Walk B continue up the green track curving round the western side of Craig Celynin. About midway, the track bears half-RIGHT, rising gently, then after a stream becomes a path, which continues alongside the wall ahead. After passing a small triangular enclosure, bear RIGHT to pass the remains of Caer Bach.

For Walk A take a path angling RIGHT through heather and gorse to cross a stream between two wall corners. Take the path close by the wall on your right – (the other is an alternative route to Maen Penddu as shown.) Follow it across open upland pasture, later turning sharp LEFT up a green track across the gorse-covered pasture towards Tal y Fan, to reach Maen Penddu. *This large flat-topped stone, almost 2 metres high, and an almost buried stone circle near-*

by, date from the 2nd millennium BC and were of likely ceremonial importance. Here, turn LEFT and follow a path to cross a stream by the second of two ruins. The path now rises and continues alongside a wall. As the wall begins to gently curve follow a path straight ahead past the end of Tal y Fan down to join Walk B at the old wall near Cae Bach. Turn RIGHT.

5 Follow the old wall on your left up to a gate and on to cross two ladder-stiles. Now follow the main path, later rejoining the wall, to cross another ladder-stile. Follow the green track down to go through two gates below Cae Coch, then cross a ladder-stile onto an old enclosed track. Follow it, soon on a steady descent, to the Youth Hostel, then continue down the steep road into Rowen. *This is the ancient route which later became part of the Roman road from Canovium fort in the Conwy valley to Segontium fort at Caernarfon. On the adjoining slopes are 2nd millennium BC standing stones and Maen y Bard Neolithic burial chamber.*

WALK 20

PEN-Y-GAER, LLYN DULYN & LLYN MELYNLLYN

DESCRIPTION An exhilarating 10 mile figure of eight walk, with extensive views, from Pen-y-gaer hillfort across a wild remote upland valley to lakes, used as reservoirs, set in two of the most dramatic corries in Snowdonia, beneath the central Carneddau mountain ridge. After visiting Pen-y-Gaer, the route follows a delightful track to cross the Afon Ddu, after which mainly level paths across wettish ground take you to Llyn Dulyn, where there is a bothy nearby for shelter. A short steep climb to Llyn Melynllyn, at 2,099 feet/640 metres, is followed by a scenic high-level track, then another takes you to a small dam, after which you follow paths, later well waymarked. Although, the walk starts high and involves little demanding climbing, it is for experienced hill walkers only, and should be avoided in poor visibility. Allow between 5-6 hours. The route can be shortened to an easier 4¼ mile walk (**B**) at the Afon Ddu.

START Pen-y-gaer [SH 744693]

DIRECTIONS From the Bedol pub in Tal-y-Bont, take the road signposted to Llanbedr-y-cennin. Go past Ye Olde Bull Inn and up the hillside. At a junction, turn left and follow the road up below the northern slopes of Pen-y-Gaer to its end, where it becomes two tracks and there is a parking area.

*P**en-y-Gaer** stands on a hill overlooking the western side of the Conwy Valley at the end of a ridge descending from the Carneddau Mountains. It is a complex fort, with one rampart on its steepest side, three ramparts elsewhere, with the inner one stone wall facing. Its defences also included the rare 'cheveux de frise'– angled pointed uneven stones embedded in the ground, seen just below its entrance from the footpath. The fort* contains about 12 roundhouse platforms. It was obviously an important centre for local tribes and probably eventually succumbed to the Romans who built a fort nearby at Caerhun in the Conwy Valley.

1 From the road end take the track leading south to cross a ladder-stile on the left. A clear path takes you to another ladder-stile providing access to the hillfort. Retrace your steps, then follow the other track, soon rising to cross an old leat and a ladder-stile. Follow the track rising gently alongside the wall beneath Penygadair, over another ladder-stile, and past one on your left (your return route). The track continues across the open slopes up to another ladder-stile, then rises steadily past another ladder-stile, where it levels out, and begins a long steady descent. *Ahead in the distance, below the Carneddau ridge, are the imposing dark crags, beneath which are the hidden lakes you seek.* After a ladder-stile, continue ahead on the now faint green track, shortly beginning another long descent. Later the track fades again as it passes through a wet area to a ladder-stile just before the Afon Ddu.

2 After crossing the river, turn LEFT and work your way across wettish ground above the river alongside the fence, which later becomes a wall, to an iron ladder-stile. (For **Walk B**, cross it and resume text at point 5.) Here, turn RIGHT to follow a path SW along the edge of a line of rushes to cross a footbridge. Continue ahead to cross an iron ladder-stile in a fence. Ultimately you are aiming to pass to the right of a small group of trees ahead. In the meanwhile, continue ahead guided by occasional small concrete 'cable below' posts. Cross a stream, then another by an old stone sheepfold and continue to a ladder-stile. Keep ahead for about 150 yards, first passing above large boulders, then over two small streams. Now bear LEFT to cross a larger stream coming from the high ground ahead and go across a shoulder into Cwm Melynllyn to join a good path passing above the Scots pines. Follow it along the valley edge to pass above Dulyn bothy to reach Llyn Dulyn. *Lying beneath the near vertical crags of Craig y Dulyn which have claimed the lives of airmen, this dark lake is said to be 189 feet deep.*

Penygadair

Pen·y·gaer

②

Afon Ddu

footbridge

⑤

Afon Melynllyn

N

0   ¼

mile

④

3 Cross the outlet and end of the lake to join a embanked path below where piped water from Llyn Melynllyn falls to be channelled into the lake, and continue on the path angling up the hillside on the line of the hidden pipeline, to eventually cross a small footbridge at the NE corner of Llyn Melynllyn. From here, a track just out of sight, heads SE to pass a ruined building. *The remains of a wheelpit and old machinery are associated with the former Melynllyn slate quarry (1867-1908) on the slopes beyond.* The track – *the former tramway serving the quarry* – continues across the mid-slopes. After a while it begins a long steady descent via two ladder-stiles, then levels out, before meandering down towards the adjoining expansive valley, with a good view of Llyn Eigiau. Just before a ladder-stile/ gate, turn sharp LEFT onto another track.

Llyn Dulyn

4 Follow the track down to cross a small dam over the Afon Melynllyn. Bear LEFT over the Afon Ddu to cross a ladder-stile. Continue ahead passing above the nearby building, then follow a clear path, initially above the river, soon rising to follow a wall up to cross the iron ladder-stile met on the outward route.

5 Cross the nearby footbridge, then follow a path contouring across the boulder-covered slope, later guided by occasional concrete posts, to cross an iron ladder-stile. The path crosses a stream, briefly runs alongside a wall, then follows a series of waymark posts to another iron ladder-stile. Continue ahead. After a wall gap, the waymarked path angles LEFT up to go through another wall-gap and on to pass a ruined hafod. At the end of a walled section, the path rises LEFT and meanders across the hillside guided by waymark posts to eventually reach a wall/ fence corner. Follow the fence to a ladder-stile, where you join your outward route.

WALK 21

BRYN CASTELL & LLYN MORWYNION

DESCRIPTION A 5½ mile (**A**) or 4½ mile (**B**) walk featuring the remote Bryn Castell hillfort, a stunning upland lake, an old slate quarry, a section of Roman Road and extensive views. The route first rises to the hidden Llyn Morwynion lying beneath mountains. Walk A goes around the lake, while Walk B heads direct to the dam. The shared route now follows a waymarked section of a Snowdonia Slate Trail to Bryn Castell, then a delightful old track up to the former 19thC Drum slate quarry. After descending an old incline it follows another track back to visit the small hillfort. Afterwards it heads south to cross the B4391 to briefly enjoy a section of Sarn Helen Roman Road before returning via Llyn Morwynion. The route includes some good tracks but also demanding tussocky/reedy terrain. Allow about 3½ hours
START Car park on B4391 [SH 735417]
DIRECTIONS The car park lies on the B4391 about 2¼ miles east of Llan Ffestiniog and ¾ mile before the junction with the B4407.

*B**ryn Castell** is a small stone walled hillfort lying in a hidden upland valley near Llan Ffestiniog. A stone rampart encircles the top of the hill, with an original blocked entrance on its northern eastern corner, and the existing later entrance a few metres further west. It was occupied from the late Iron Age into the Roman period. It was completely excavated from 1979-85 and the rampart and interior stone buildings partly reconstructed. It contained many structures, including two stake-walled round huts and the remains of iron-smelting furnaces, along with a stone anvil and related tools.*

I Turn RIGHT along the road to cross a stile opposite. Follow a path up to a an old green track – *with a view of Llyn Morwynion ahead.* (For **Walk B** follow it left through a wall to the bend of a stony track. Follow the

track to the dam of Llyn Morwynin and turn left along a side track to two stone buildings, then bear right over a stream and follow the fence to a small gate and waymark post beyond at point 3.) For **Walk A** follow a path ahead through reeds, soon taking its right fork to the corner of the lake. Continue with a path along the edge of the lake to a stream and kissing gate in the lake corner.

2 Go through the kissing gate and along the lake's edge. In its next corner follow a path to cross a stream and across tussocky/reedy ground. The path now rises then crosses the slope, initially about 20 yards above the lake edge. It continues across reedy ground to join an incoming quad track. Soon – *with good views west to the dam of Llyn Stwlan set high amongst the Moelwyns and to the Llyn Peninsula* – follow a path leading LEFT to pass above a fence at the recessed lake corner and on with a wall to a waymark post, where you join the Snowdonia Slate Trail.

3 Follow the path on a steady descent a few yards from the wall beneath crags and past a small stone building to another waymark post. The path descends close to high ground on your right past nearby old quarry workings, soon bending right through reeds to a good cross-path. Follow it LEFT down to a stone sheepfold and turn RIGHT past a ladder-stile below. Now work your way across a wettish reedy area to another ladder-stile ahead. Follow the fence on your left, soon through bracken, to cross a stile. Just below turn RIGHT beside the boundary past Garreglwyd cottage to a waymark post. Bear RIGHT up and across the field and over an old boundary corner. Go along the edge of the next large reedy/tussocky field to a stile amongst bracken by a waymarked fence section. Follow a path leading LEFT, passing just beneath high ground, towards

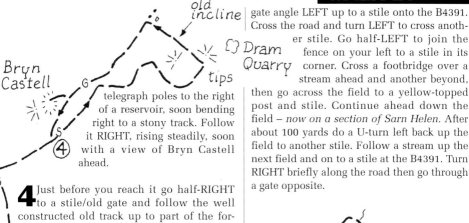

telegraph poles to the right of a reservoir, soon bending right to a stony track. Follow it RIGHT, rising steadily, soon with a view of Bryn Castell ahead.

4 Just before you reach it go half-RIGHT to a stile/old gate and follow the well constructed old track up to part of the former Drum quarry – *worked from the 1860s*

gate angle LEFT up to a stile onto the B4391. Cross the road and turn LEFT to cross another stile. Go half-LEFT to join the fence on your left to a stile in its corner. Cross a footbridge over a stream ahead and another beyond, then go across the field to a yellow-topped post and stile. Continue ahead down the field – *now on a section of Sarn Helen.* After about 100 yards do a U-turn left back up the field to another stile. Follow a stream up the next field and on to a stile at the B4391. Turn RIGHT briefly along the road then go through a gate opposite.

to the late 1880s, employing 30 men at its peak in 1872. Now descend the remains of an old incline to a track. Follow it LEFT back towards Bryn Castell to a stile/gate and a track junction just beyond beneath the hillfort. Go up its northern slope to the fort's entrance. After exploring the fort and enjoying the views, return to the track junction and turn RIGHT along the track, soon on your outward route. Follow the track down and on past the reservoir and water treatment works. Continue along its access track to cross over the river. Just beyond a small utility building up on your left and before a

5 Turn RIGHT up the signposted path on a faint green track, soon bending left with the incoming fence which you follow to a ladder-stile to join your outward route. Follow it back up to the waymark post at point 3. The waymarked Slate Trail leads to the dam (used by Walk B), but a more interesting way is to cross a protected section of fence at the end of the recessed corner of the lake and follow a path over a stream and on across the dam. Go along its stony access track and when it bends sharp right turn LEFT along an old reedy green track, then descend your outward path to the road.

DINAS EMRYS

DESCRIPTION A 2¼ mile waymarked National Trust trail to Dinas Emrys, an ancient fortified site on a prominent small wooded volcanic hill overlooking the Gwynant valley, celebrated in Welsh folklore, offering great views. It returns the same way, then follows other waymarked trails back to the start. Allow about 1½ hours.

START Craflwyn National Trust car park [SH 600490]

DIRECTIONS Craflwyn lies just off the A498 about 1 mile from Beddgelert.

A *ccording to legend Dinas Emrys was the location of warlord Vortigern's 5th C castle, home of the red dragon seen on the Welsh flag, and associated with Merlin the Magician. Whatever the truth evidence shows that this strategic site overlooking an ancient route through the mountains has been occupied from the Iron Age, through the Roman period to Medieval times. It contains the remains of a complex stone fort, with encircling stone ramparts. On its summit are the restored stone foundations of a late 12thC castle keep, probably built as a symbol of the power of the Princes of Gwynedd. Below it is a medieval cistern fed by a spring. The supply of fresh water was one of the main reasons why this hilltop has been fortified through the ages.*

1 The trail heads along the driveway soon taking its right fork to the hall. It bends right with the driveway to a gate on the left and continues to an information board with a good view of Dinas Emrys. Return to the bend of the driveway, go past the side of the hall and up steps to a gate. Turn RIGHT up the stony track. Soon angle LEFT up a path to a gate and up to a T-junction with green/blue trails.

2 Turn RIGHT up the path. Soon the trails part. Keep ahead down to a narrow gap in a wall corner, across a footbridge over a stream to a small gate. The path soon descends to cross a slab stone bridge over a river by a delightful waterfall and deep pool. The path continues briefly above the river, then turns LEFT beside a wall, rises steadily and splits. The trail takes the right fork beside the wall to a ladder-stile, crosses a small wooded knoll, then descends to a stile and continues past a post to rise between rocks. It then heads along the tree-covered rocky ridge past a great view of Llyn Gwynant and up through the hillfort past the castle keep foundations on the summit to the hill's edge for new views. Return to point 2, then follow the green/blue trails down through woodland to the car park.

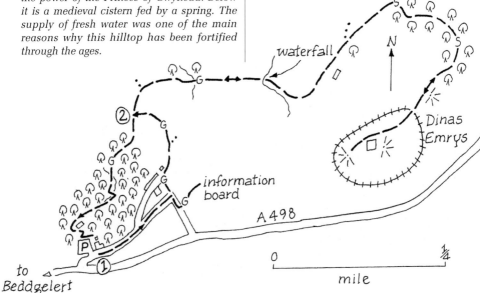

34

DINAS TY-DU

DESCRIPTION A 2½ mile walk exploring the countryside above Llanberis in Snowdonia, featuring a waterfall and the small Iron Age hill-fort of Dinas Ty-Du on a prominent hill (1050 ft / 320 metres), offering panoramic views. Allow about 2 hours.
START Dolbadaran Hotel, High Street, Llanberis [SH 579601]
DIRECTIONS The High Street is accessible from a choice of car parks.

*L*lanberis *developed as a quarry-ing village beside Llyn Padarn, but later became a popular Victorian tourist resort, attracted by guided climbs up Snowdon. Its popularity increased after 1869 with the opening of a branch railway line from Caernarfon, then the building of the Snowdon Mountain Railway in 1896. Another major attraction is the National Slate Museum, which occupies old Victorian quarry workshops, that once served the massive Dinorwig quarry carved out of the mountainside, and which become one of the largest in the world during the 19thC. The museum, which provides a fascinating insight into the slate industry, is free and open throughout the year and well worth a visit.*

*D*inas Ty-Du *is a small Iron Age hillfort standing on the top of a prominent hill (about 90 metres) overlooking Llanberis on the edge of the Snowdonia National Park. It was defended by steep slopes and a single rampart, but lacks evidence of long term occupation. It may have provided short term refuge for occupants of nearby roundhouses.*

From the Hotel head south east, then at Snowdon Garage turn RIGHT along a road past the church. Soon after it bends left take a signposted path through a gate on the right up to a kissing gate. Follow the path past a cottage then up through trees to another

kissing gate and on to briefly join a track. Take a path angling RIGHT from a telegraph pole, then go up a minor road. Just past a cottage go through a kissing gate on the left over the Snowdon railway line for a view of the Ceunant Mawr waterfall. Continue up the road past a track to a kissing gate ahead on the bend. Go up the field edge to a waymarked path junction by a wall corner/kissing gate. Go across the wide path and on up to a kissing gate by a stream. Follow the stream up to another kissing gate then the wall up to a road by Hafod Uchaf. Go up the road to a gate onto a track.

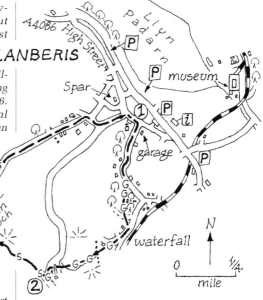

2 Turn RIGHT to a ladder-stile/gate and follow the delightful bridleway across the hillside to cross a bridge over the Afon Goch and on to a minor road. Follow it up past a ruin, then continue up a green track. At a ladder-stile follow the wall RIGHT to a kissing gate. Go up to the top of the narrow hill containing the remains of Dinas Ty-Du. After enjoying the extensive views return to the kissing gate, then follow the path east down to another kissing gate and down the hillside to the road. Follow it down to Llanberis.

WALK 24

BWRDD ARTHUR

DESCRIPTION A 5 mile meandering and undulating walk to one of the largest hillforts on Anglesey, Bwrdd Arthur, an Open Access area, offering panoramic views, returning on the Wales Coast Path (WCP). Allow about 3 hours.
START Traeth Coch (east) beach car park [SH 568806]
DIRECTIONS The car park with toilets and seasonal cafe is reached by a steep minor road from the northern end of Llanddona.

*B*wrdd *Arthur hillfort, also known as Din Sylwy, stands on a small table top .limestone hill (538 feet/164 metres) a prominent landmark overlooking Red Wharf Bay. Built in the Iron Age it is enclosed by a single stone wall of limestone blocks set above steep slopes, with entrances to the west and south. Roman finds, including coins, pottery and broaches, indicate it was occupied during the later Roman period. Beneath its eastern slopes is the small 15thC church of Llanfihangel Din Sylwy. Quarries on the nearby cliffs provided limestone for the Menai Suspension Bridge.*

1 Follow the road west, soon bending inland. After the road rises turn LEFT on a signposted path along a track past a cottage to a kissing gate and another ahead. Go across the top of a field to a hidden kissing gate near the corner. Follow the next large field edge down to a kissing gate onto a stony track. Turn RIGHT up a long tree-lined path by a stream to a house. Go past its right-hand side and a caravan up to a kissing gate just beyond an old ruin. Follow the clear path ahead up the hillside, soon enclosed, past a waymarked path junction at a good viewpoint to a kissing gate onto a road. Go up it. At the T-junction turn LEFT down the road. On the bend take the signposted bridleway through Ysgubor Penrallt's gated entrance and along a stony track past the outbuilding/cottage, then bend LEFT down the main track through trees and over a stream. Continue with the tree-lined path, shortly bending left to eventually emerge at the entrance to Hafod Wen. Go down its concrete driveway.

2 Just before Tros yr Afon turn RIGHT up steps and follow the enclosed path up to join a narrow hedged track which rises to a road at a good viewpoint. Go up the road and past a transmitter mast – *now with a view of Bwrdd Arthur*. At the junction turn LEFT. Follow the road past a stile on the bend and on beneath Bwrdd Arthur to a kissing gate at the junction. Follow a waymarked path up onto Bwrd Arthur's southern edge. From here the path extends to both the trig point and eastern ramparts for great views. Retrace your steps to cross the stile on the bend of the road.

3 Follow the signposted path across Bwrdd Arthur's lower western slopes, then take a path on the left down to a kissing gate to join the original section of the WCP. Follow the kissing gated path along the long field edge and down into National Trust owned Bryn Offa, then past a seat and down the gorse-covered hillside. Go across a green track and down a new stepped section of the WCP to a kissing gate on the cliffs. The WCP continues to a lane then descends it to a small gate by Godreddi Mawr. Follow the kissing-gated

36

WCP through fields, then down steps and along the edge of the rocky shore to a footbridge over a stream. Return along the road or the sandy beach if low tide (a flagpole will guide you to access points by the car park).

WALK 25
DINAS GYNFOR

DESCRIPTION A 4½ mile walk through attractive countryside and a return along Anglesey's stunning cliff-top Wales Coast Path via Dinas Gynfor fort, a commemorative tower, former porcelain works at Porth Llanlleaina, and 12th C Llanbadrig Church. Allow about 3 hours.
START Cemaes Bay beach car park
[SH 376937]
DIRECTIONS The car park (also Llanbadrig church/Gadlys Hotel) is signposted off the A5025 just east of Cemaes. Follow the narrow road past The Gadlys, then at the junction turn left down to the car park.

Dinas Gynfor is a large promontory coastal Iron Age hillfort near Cemaes. It stands about 200 feet on a headland, protected by steep cliffs on three sides and crags, a limestone block wall and ditch across its steep sloping landward side.

1 Go back up the road to the junction. Turn RIGHT then take a signposted path over a stone stile to a kissing gate. The path continues beneath the bracken-covered slope and across a small field to gates in the corner. Go along the next field edge to gates, then along the edge of a nearby house's lawn and over its access track to a small gate. Follow the path through the field ahead, a boundary gap, and another field down to a footbridge/small gate, then up to a road.

2 Follow it RIGHT. When it bends right go through a kissing gate on the left. Go up and along the field edge and over Llanlleiana's stony access track. Go down the narrow green track ahead, then a field towards Dinas Gynfor and across a causeway over a reedy marsh. Just beyond an old gateway/concrete ladder-stile you meet a cross path. Follow it RIGHT up across the bracken-covered hillside. At a waymarked WCP junction turn LEFT and climb to the top of Dinas Gynfor. Continue to the small tower – *built to commemorate Edward VII's coronation in 1901. The hillfort's ramparts can be seen on the inland side.* Soon the path descends steeply to the ruins and chimney of the former Llanlleiana porcelain works – *which used China clay from the hillside, and the tiny cove for shipping during the 19thC until its closure in 1920.*

3 Now follow the undulating WCP along the impressive cliffs to Llanbadrig church – *founded in 440 AD it is the only one in Wales dedicated to St Patrick of Ireland, allegedly after he sheltered in a cave here following being shipwrecked.* After a gate at its wall corner go up the slope ahead past a seat and down to a cross-path. Follow it to the tip of the headland, then return along its south side, rising above Porth Padrig, then bending left to a car-park by the church. Go down the road to a kissing gate then follow the cliff-top WCP to the start.

DINAS DINLLE

DESCRIPTION A 3 mile walk along a section of the Wales Coast Path to the landmark Iron Age Dinas Dinlle hillfort, overlooking the small seaside holiday village of the same name, with the option of returning along the beach if tide permits, or vice versa. The fort, owned by the National Trust, is open for visits and has an interpretation panel. Although only about 100 ft/ 30 metres high it offers panoramic coastal views. Before returning you can enjoy refreshments at a choice of cafés, bars, and fish & chip shop. The walk can easily be shortened by starting from different beach car parks.

START Dinas Dinlle beach car park by the corner of Caernarfon Airport. [SH 432583]

DIRECTIONS Turn off the A499 Pwllheli road direct or via Llandwrog to Dinas Dinlle. Head north along the shoreline road to the car park on its far bend.

*D**inas Dinlle** lies at the northern end of the Lleyn Peninsula just south of the Menai Strait. The hillfort overlooks the holiday village and its lovely beach, sandy at mid to low tide. The hillfort was built on an outcrop of glacial deposit surrounded by salt marshes over 2500 years ago. It would have been a prominent and intimidating feature in that landscape. Over time the western side of the fort has been eroded by the encroaching sea, and continues today. Remaining are two lines of ramparts with a ditch between, with an entrance on its southeast side. Its inner ramparts were probably originally topped by a timber fence. Small depressions indicate possible round houses and a mound may be a Bronze Age barrow or the base of a Roman pharos (lighthouse). Chance finds show occupation in the late Roman period. Dinas Dinlle is associated with a medieval Mabinogi tale where it was the home of Lleu Llaw Gyffes – hence 'din' meaning 'fort' and 'Lle' short for 'Lleu'.*

Follow the surfaced Wales Coast Path south by the shore to the bend of the nearby road, then along the narrow promenade

by the pebbly foreshore to the fish and chip shop at its end. Go past its side onto the beach then bend left to an information board on the hillfort and a small gate above.

2 Follow the wooden slotted path angling across the hillfort's northern slope, then turn LEFT along the inner ramparts, with lower ones below, round to a clifftop fence overlooking the beach. Continue down a path and along the low cliffs past a gate giving access to the beach up to another gate. Pause to enjoy the views then return onto the hillfort to complete its circuit and reach its highest point offering good views north along the beach to Anglesey. Descend to the entry gate then either return along the Wales Coast Path or the beach after enjoying refreshments.

WALK 27

TRE'R CEIRI

DESCRIPTION A 4 mile walk to Tre'r Ceiri, on the Llyn Peninsula, one of the best .preserved and most spectacular hillforts .in Britain, returning via the small crags of Caergribin, both providing extensive views. Allow about 2½ hours.

START Car Park above Nant Gwrtheyrn [SH 353441]

DIRECTIONS At the crossroads in Llithfaen, turn off the B4417 on a minor road signposted to Nant Gwrtheyrn to reach the large car park by a forest and stone sculpture.

Tre'r Ceiri (Town of the Giants) hill-fort stands at a height of 1590 feet/485 metres on the eastern peak of Yr Eifll. The fort is encircled by a massive stone rampart wall, over 3 metres high, with two main entrances. It contains an early Bronze Age burial cairn at its summit and the remains of over 150 stone huts, some with two or three rooms. The fort was supplied with water from a spring just outside. It is surrounded by small terraced enclosures, probably used for animals and cultivation. The fort was used during the Iron Age and throughout the Roman occupation, when it became a settlement of possibly 400 inhabitants. Most of the finds, including an elaborate gold plated brooch, date to the Romano-British period.

Follow the road back to the second multi-finger post and turn LEFT to follow the wall up across open ground, later descending with the wall to the entrance to Brynffynon cottage. Here go half-LEFT on a wide path to join a narrow green track. Follow it LEFT up to a waymarked path junction. Just beyond bend half-RIGHT up to a stream, then follow a stony path up through heather/bracken to

a kissing gate. Continue with the path past a waymarked path junction to another kissing gate, then follow the path up through heather. At a path junction by a small post keep ahead up a stonier path to an information board beneath the hillfort's south-west entrance. Enter the fort and follow its massive rampart in a clockwise direction, past its impressive western entrance to complete a full interior exploration. Leave the fort and return down to the kissing gate. Keep ahead past a waymarked side path.

2 About 100 yards further, take the next path on the left to the northern end of the small rocky ridge of Caergribin. The path then bends right and climbs onto small crags. Return down the path and just before a line of boulders, turn LEFT along a sketchy path, soon bending left beneath a large crag, then splitting. Here turn RIGHT past another small crag, then follow a good path, keeping with its left fork and soon bending right to the kissing gate to rejoin your outward route. Follow the path ahead down to a stream, then a wide green path angling right to the waymarked path junction passed earlier. Here turn RIGHT up the hillside. The path rises steadily past other cross-paths, later levelling out at a crossroad of paths at a waymark post. Turn LEFT and follow the increasingly wide path down to the multi-finger post.

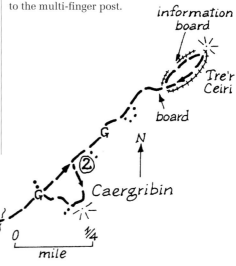

39

WALK 28

CASTELL CAERAU

DESCRIPTION A 3½ mile walk to a small hillfort site above the village of Garndolbenmaen, north-west of Porthmadog, and a climb up the small hill of Craig-y- Garn (1191 ft/363metres) that overlooks it. The route follows scenic roads up through an attractive landscape of small walled enclosures to join a delightful old walled bridleway beneath Craig-y-Garn, an Open Access area. The short climb to its summit from stone sheepfolds on good paths is worth it for the breathtaking views. Paths take you to Castell Caerau and back to the bridleway, before a road descent to the village. Allow about 2 hours.

START Garndolbenmaen [SH 497442]

DIRECTIONS Garndolbenmaen is signposted from the A487 about 4½ miles west of Tremadog. At a staggered crossroad In the village centre by the village hall park on the road opposite an old chapel.

Castell Caerau is a small walled fort standing on a rocky knoll beneath the southern slopes of Craig-y-Garn near the village of Garndolbenmaen. It is said to be prehistoric but little is known about it. It may be medieval if associated with the castle mound at Dolbenmaen by the A487 just to the south.

1 Go up the No Through Road opposite the old chapel. Follow it past a side road and up past dwellings, then another side road. At the next junction turn RIGHT rising more steeply up the road, then bending to a great viewpoint looking west along the Llyn Peninsula. Here turn RIGHT through a gate and continue along a road to another gate. Turn RIGHT on a signposted bridleway/stony track to a gate. The bridleway continues along a delightful old walled track past nearby Ffridd Newydd cottage.

2 Just beyond a gate cross a stone stile on the left. Follow a path ahead up and across the heather terrain to a wall by sheepfolds beneath craggy Craig-y-Garn. Cross a ladder-stile and go through the gated sheepfold. Follow a path soon angling right and climbing up towards the col between Craig-y-Garn's two peaks. Soon after being joined by another path it splits. Continue up the wider right fork beneath the higher peak on the right and along the right edge of a flat tussocky area. It then bends up right. As it levels out take a path leading right up to the summit, containing three small stone wind shelters – *for which I was very grateful on the day I was there!* Return to cross the ladder-stile by the sheepfolds and turn LEFT.

3 Follow a path southwards by or near the wall, at its corner bending down towards Castell Caerau. Just before the lower wall corner the path angles right to join the wall. Continue close beside it to go through a gap in it. Follow a path to this ancient site intersected by a wall. Return to pass through the wall gap then continue west with the wall. At a partly collapsed section, about 50 yards before the wall corner and trees, take a path leading RIGHT up to pass a hidden wall corner just above. The good path continues beside the meandering wall to the stone stile at point 2. Continue along the walled bridleway to a gate by a cottage. Go down its access road then follow a minor road down past a side road to the junction with your outward road. Follow it back to the start.

40

WALK 29

MOEL Y GEST

DESCRIPTION A 3½ mile (**A**) or 3 mile (**B**) walk up to the site of a Iron Age hillfort on the western summit of Moel y Gest (863 feet 263 metres), a prominent isolated rugged hill overlooking Porthmadog, offering spectacular views. Walk A takes a longer approach to the bwlch at point 2 but offers a view of Cist Cerrig, a megalithic burial chamber, whilst Walk B is more direct. The route continues up to the col between the two peaks of Moel y Gest then heads west along the rough boulder-covered ridge up to the summit – a more demanding section with occasional easy scrambling. Afterwards you have an option to climb to Moel y Gest's second summit. Allow about 2½ hours.

START Morfa Bychan Road [SH 556378]

DIRECTIONS From Porthmadog's main street take the road signposted to Morfa Bwychan/Black Rock Sands. After passing the turning for Borth-y-Gest. it rises to the entrance to Blackrock Llama Centre on the right, with parking for about three cars on the grass verge just before it.

Moel y Gest hillfort is defended by natural steep slopes on three sides and has a small walled enclosure. It contains many white quartz stones, possibly used as slingstones.

I Cross the ladder-stile at the entrance to Blackrock Llama Centre. Go along the stony track past a small lake to a gate. (For **Walk B** follow the waymarked path up through gorse to a gate, then an old walled green track to a stone stile/gate at the bwlch.) For **Walk A** continue along the track up to its end at Ty'n-y-mynydd. Follow a path to a kissing gate ahead and down to join another descending from the left. Just before a gateway in an old wall below turn RIGHT along a faint path by the wall to its

end. The path then rises ahead by another wall to a waymarked stone stile/old gate. *In two fields away to your left are three large stones, the remains of Cist Cerrig, whose covering cairn is missing.* Follow a path through a small area of gorse, soon bending down to a gateway in an old wall. Go up a green track beside the wall, soon moving away and fading. Go up the grass slope a few yards further to a single gorse bush on the left. Here turn LEFT to join a path in a nearby gap in the gorse. It rises to a cross path and wall just above a small gate. Follow the path RIGHT beside the wall up to a stone stile/gate at the bwlch.

2 From here a path leads to an old gateway in a nearby wall and to a gap in the larger wall ahead. The path then rises in the same direction across the slope to the col between Moel y Gest's two peaks onto the main ridge. Now make your way westwards across the boulder and rough grass covered ridge up to its broad summit containing a trig point and the remains of its fort. Return to the col for an optional climb to Moel y Gest's second summit before returning to point 2. Descend an old walled green track to a gate then a path to join your outward stony track.

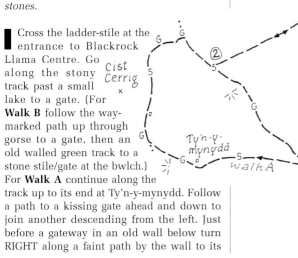

WALK 30

CARN FADRYN & GARN BACH

DESCRIPTION A 3¹/₃ mile (**A**) walk in the heart of the Llyn Peninsula, featuring the prominent heather and rock covered hill of Carn Fadryn (1216 feet/371 metres) offering extensive views from its summit containing the remains of both an Iron Age hillfort and a 12thC castle. It also includes the nearby hill of Garn Bach (921 feet/281 metres). Although not high, Carn Fadryn is mountainous in character, but a meandering path makes for an enjoyable ascent. Avoid in poor visibility. Allow about 2½ hours. Also included is 3 mile walk (**B**) around the lower slopes of Carn Fadryn, which can be combined with an ascent of both tops.
START Old Chapel, Garnfadryn [SH 278345]
DIRECTIONS Garnfadryn lies south of Morfa Nefyn. There is a car park by the former chapel.

Carn Fadryn is crowned by a large hill-fort developed in two phases. The second fort enclosed by stone walls was larger than the first, with entrances to the north and south. It contains the remains of various stone-walled huts. Similar remains can be found on Carn Fadryn's steep slopes. A small stone enclosure at the summit's highest point is the ruin of small motte castle reputedly built along with others in the late 12thC by the sons of the Welsh Prince Owain Gwynedd. What views across the Llyn the various occupants of the hilltop enjoyed!

I From the end of the chapel house go up an enclosed access track. When it bends right follow a path up to a gate by a small covered reservoir beneath Carn Fadryn. Turn RIGHT along the path near the boundary, soon rising steadily to a viewpoint looking east to nearby Pwllheli and the distant mountains of Snowdonia. The path then angles away from the wall. (For **Walk B** continue beside the wall to cross a stile in it and resume text at point 3.) The path meanders steadily up the southern slopes of Carn Fadryn, changing in character from wide short cut grass to stone stepped. Eventually the path passes through stone ramparts into the hillfort's flattish interior.

2 There are a choice of three paths to the summit trig point as shown. The clearest follows cairns through the centre of the fort. I suggest you follow a sketchy path by the nearby small craggy heather western ridge to the trig point – *offering superb views along Llyn's both coasts, and to the Snowdonia mountains.* Return briefly down the path, then follow another towards the fort's flat centre to pass a large cairn to join a clear path heading south to the fort entrance. Descend the hillside, then just before the final bend, take another path angling LEFT down to cross a stile in the wall below.

3 Go across open pasture towards a kissing gate ahead, then bear LEFT along a path, soon joining another, which you follow down to cross a waymarked stone stile just to the left of a gate in the wall ahead. (For **Walk B** cross the nearby ladder-stile. Turn RIGHT briefly alongside the fence, then angle away across upland pasture to a gap in the old wall ahead. Go up the next field to join the wall ahead where it meets an old low boundary. Follow the wall up to pass a nearby small crag offering superb views, then down the steep slope to cross a ladder-stile over it. Go half-RIGHT across the large field to the wall ahead. Follow it LEFT, soon through reeds then bracken to a stile. Go along the next field edge to another stile. Now follow the wall along the forest edge (bracken in high summer) to a post on the wall where you cross a stone stile into the second adjoining field. Cross the nearby stile. Now follow the wall through two fields (stiles) past Coed Garn Fadryn and across bracken-covered pasture to its corner. Go past the nearby ruin to join a green track. After passing a cottage it rises beneath the western slopes of Carn Fadryn, later joining a road, which continues up to a junction. Keep ahead back to the start.) For **Walk A** turn RIGHT and follow the wall up to the craggy top of Garn Bach. Follow a path to the next small rocky top, then down the slope near the wall to go

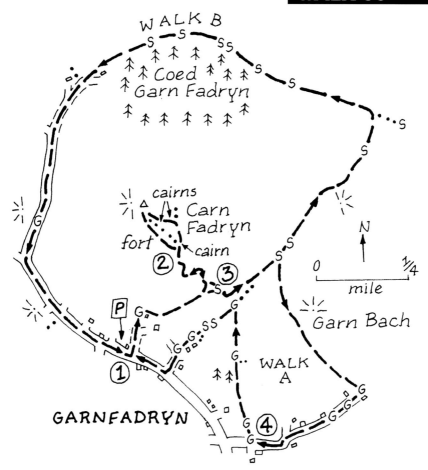

through a waymarked small iron gate in it above Pen-y-Caerau cottage. Follow its access track, then a lane past cottages – all the way to the village road for a simple return if preferred.

4 At a farm entrance, go through a kissing gate on the right. Follow the path along the edge of two small fields to a small gate. Continue along the next field edge and up a faint green track. Soon leave it to walk alongside the perimeter fence of a small wood, then follow a waymarked path ahead to a kissing gate and on beside an old wall. At its corner continue ahead up the long field to a kissing gate in the wall ahead seen on your outward route. Turn LEFT .to follow a path

down across bracken covered pasture. After about 70 yards continue down its right fork to cross two stiles in a recessed boundary corner ahead. Go down the enclosed path to a waymarked gate and down the left-hand edge of two fields to a kissing gate, then follow an access track down to the village road. Turn RIGHT back to the start.

KEY TO THE MAPS

- ➜ Walk route and direction
- ――― Metalled road
- --- Unsurfaced road
- •••• Footpath/route adjoining walk route
- ∿➔ River/stream
- ♠ ♧ Trees
- ▬▬ Railway
- **G** Gate
- **S** Stile
- **F.B.** Footbridge
- ⊻ Viewpoint
- P Parking
- T Telephone

THE COUNTRYSIDE CODE

- Be safe – plan ahead and follow any signs
- Leave gates and property as you find them
- Protect plants and animals, and take your litter home
- Keep dogs under close control
- Consider other people

Open Access
Some routes cross areas of land where walkers have the legal right of access under The CRoW Act 2000 introduced in May 2005. Access can be subject to restrictions and closure for land management or safety reasons for up to 28 days a year.
Please respect any notices.

About the author David Berry

David is an experienced walker with a love of the countryside and an interest in local history. He is the author of a series of walks guidebooks covering North Wales, where he has lived and worked for many years. He has written for Walking Wales and Ramblers Walk magazine, worked as a Rights of Way surveyor across North Wales and served as a member of Denbighshire Local Access Forum. Whether on a riverside ramble, mountain or long distance walk, he greatly appreciates the beauty, culture and history of the landscape and hopes that his comprehensive guidebooks will encourage people to explore on foot its diverse scenery and rich heritage. For more information visit: www.davidberrywalks.co.uk

Published by **Kittiwake Books Limited**
3 Glantwymyn Village Workshops, Glantwymyn, Machynlleth, Montgomeryshire SY20 8LY

© Text & map research: David Berry 2018
© Maps & illustrations: Kittiwake-Books Ltd 2018
Drawings by Morag Perrott
Cover photos: Main: View from Moel y Gaer (Walk 1).
Inset: Tre'r Ceiri (Walk 27). David Berry.

Care has been taken to be accurate. However neither the author nor the publisher can accept responsibility for any errors which may appear, or their consequences. If you are in any doubt about access, check before you proceed.

Printed by Mixam UK.

ISBN: **978 1 908748 55 3**